Unmatched Grit

Adam Parsch

Published by Adam Parsch, 2025.

UNMATCHED GRIT

First edition. March 15, 2025.

Copyright © 2025 Adam Parsch.

ISBN: 979-8230899938

Written by Adam Parsch.

Dedication

To the Father, Son, and Holy Spirit:

None of this would be possible without the immeasurable love and grace of the Lord our God. Thank You, Heavenly Father, for Your unwavering guidance, unconditional love, and constant presence. Trusting in You has allowed me to be a beacon of light in this dark world, and I am forever humbled by Your mercy. May Your will be done, not mine, but Yours, forever and ever. Amen.

To my beautiful wife, Stephanie:

Thank you for your endless love, support, and unwavering belief in me. From the moment we met, you've challenged me to be the best version of myself—pushing me to grow, learn, and evolve in ways I never imagined. You are my inspiration, and this book is as much yours as it is mine.

To my parents, Alan and Nancy Parsch:

Thank you for providing me with a foundation of love and opportunity. Your encouragement and sacrifices made it possible for me to explore this world and chase my dreams. I am forever grateful for your endless support, and I wouldn't be here today without you.

To my sister, Christy Conn, and brother-in-law, Eric Conn: Your insights and advice have made this journey all the more meaningful. Thank you for being an extra set of eyes and ears along the way. Your input has been invaluable, and I am deeply grateful for your presence in my life.

To the remaining members of my family, friends, and coworkers:

Whether you realize it or not, each of you has played a part in bringing me to this moment. Our relationships—big and small—have shaped me and led me to this point. I thank you all from the bottom of my heart for your support, encouragement, and the role you've played in my journey.

Preface:

In recent years, the Detroit Lions have undergone a remarkable transformation—not just in terms of their performance on the field but also in the very culture of their organization. Under the leadership of owner Sheila Hamp, General Manager Brad Holmes, and Head Coach Dan Campbell, the Lions have become a shining example of what it means to build a positive workplace environment. Their journey, filled with challenges and triumphs, is an inspiring testament to the power of faith and leadership. This book takes us through their story, examining how their commitment to Christlike principles has reshaped their culture, leading to success on and off the field.

However, this book is not just about football but about understanding what defines workplace culture and why it matters. The scope of our exploration delves into the intricacies of creating a healthy, thriving organizational environment. A place where trust, unity, and service to one another prevail. We will look closely at the Detroit Lions' current transformation and compare it with organizations that have struggled due to toxic leadership and misguided priorities (Maleka, 2023). Along the way, we will reflect deeply on how the teachings of Jesus Christ align with these values and can transform any workplace—whether in sports or any other industry.

Growing up in a Midwestern, blue-collar environment instilled a deep appreciation for hard work, discipline, and family values. Embracing Christianity was an integral part of life. However, it was not always something I fully accepted. Most Sundays, we attended church because Mom and Dad made us go, but faith and the teachings of Jesus Christ became more apparent over time. This personal journey and my experiences living and working across the United States provided valuable insights into the significant cultural and lifestyle differences that can profoundly impact workplace dynamics. These insights form the basis of our exploration in this book.

Traveling throughout the continental United States also offered a broadened perspective while exploring various parts of the world, including Spain, Italy, Fiji, Mexico, and Canada, resulting in a deepened understanding of how people from different backgrounds approach life. These diverse perspectives can impact personality and, ultimately, workplace culture (Saha et al., 2020). A constant pursuit of learning, particularly regarding the source of truth, has led to two years of reading the Bible cover to cover. This journey has facilitated the exploration of the foundational teachings of Jesus Christ and his vision of a universal church that transcends all boundaries and embraces diversity with love and respect.

In a world where successful, positive workplace cultures are becoming increasingly important, this book will show us why the research behind these changes is vital (Raj, 2023). The in-depth analysis of the Detroit Lions' transformation and the comparison with other organizations will provide valuable insights into the importance of a thriving workplace culture. By evaluating the Lions' culture through the lens of Christ-centered leadership, this book aims to shed light on how any organization—no matter its challenges—can make a decisive shift toward a more positive, Christ-centered environment.

Let us embark on a thought-provoking journey and open our hearts to the possibility that workplace culture and the teachings of Jesus Christ can not only coexist but should complement one another for lasting impact. Throughout this exploration, it is crucial to actively consider how these insights impact one's work environment and personal life. Active engagement with these ideas will enrich your understanding and contribute to the ongoing conversation about workplace culture and faith.

Chapter 1: The Detroit Lions: A Culture Reborn

Maya Angelou once said, "You can't really know where you're going until you know where you've been." Lawyers frequently use this quote in the courtroom to argue that past events can predict future outcomes. It is a powerful sentiment, but it is uncertain if Maya Angelou ever met the Detroit Lions. If she had, she might have had second thoughts about the certainty of that statement.

The Lions' story does not quite follow that predictable pattern. Established in 1930 as the Portsmouth Spartans, the team moved to Detroit in 1934 and became the Detroit Lions. In their early years, the franchise was a model of success, winning multiple NFL championships in the 1950s under coach Buddy Parker. The Lions were a force to be reckoned with, a beacon of excellence in the league. Nevertheless, they veered off course for reasons that defy any neat narrative. Success on the field did not translate to long-term organizational stability. Leadership changes, management issues, and financial instability began to plague the franchise, and what had once been a dominant force became, for many years, a struggling team mired in dysfunction (NFL Football Operations, n.d.).

This early success, followed by prolonged mediocrity, creates an interesting tension in the Lions' history—a disharmony far from the typical tale of decline. Moreover, that is precisely where this story gets interesting.

In 1963, the Ford family purchased the Lions, with William Clay Ford Sr. becoming the principal owner (NFL Football Operations, n.d.). This marked the beginning of an era that saw both on-field success and significant off-field struggles. While the team remained in the Ford family for decades, the lack of sustained leadership and strategic vision began to show through in the team's performance, and their inability to develop a thriving workplace culture became apparent.

The 1970s to the 2010s were tough years for the Lions. Despite several successful individual seasons, the team failed to build a consistent winning formula, suffering from constant leadership changes, poor management decisions, and internal instability. The Lions often struggled with a fractured front office and ineffective coaching hires (Payton). This tumultuous environment created an organization marked by frustration and a lack of trust between ownership, management, and players.

Throughout this challenging period, the workplace culture of the Detroit Lions was frequently characterized as toxic—a sentiment echoed by anyone familiar with the team's history (Thomas, 2020). Group one, the die-hard Lions fans who know the story all too well, are familiar with the team's struggles. They will recognize the lack of organizational clarity, where key leadership positions often seem to change without a clear vision for the future. Like those who tried to step in and turn things around, coaches often struggled to impose a coherent direction. On the field, the players felt the same frustration—team morale suffered, and the absence of a healthy organizational structure led to dissatisfaction across various roles. Disillusioned with the team's internal workings, many players left with negative opinions that lasted long after their tenure.

For group two, those who celebrate the transformative power of faith and view religion as a means of turning "evil" into "good," the Lions' story might resonate deeply. Just as we see in the teachings of Jesus Christ, the capacity for redemption and transformation is always present, even in the darkest circumstances. In the Lions' case, this transformation took a long time to take root, but the possibility of change was always there. Leaders, like Head Coach Dan Campbell, embody the faith virtues of patience, humility, and grace. They understood that even the most toxic environments can be redeemed through servant leadership, just as Christ taught that love and service are the authentic marks of leadership. Campbell's willingness to rebuild the culture—on and off the field—aligns with the Christian notion of forgiveness and renewal, where change is often slow but always possible with the right heart and vision.

For group three, those critically examining ways to improve workplace culture, the Lions' evolution is a powerful case study. They will recognize that a healthy workplace starts with a clear leadership that fosters open communication, trust, and a sense of belonging. The Lions' initial lack of direction and ongoing leadership turnover created an environment where morale and frustration were low. However, as they began implementing a new framework centered on shared values and trust—much like any successful business or organization—their turnaround showed that focusing on leadership characteristics like emotional intelligence, empathy, and accountability could create lasting change. The Lions' example proves that, much like in any workplace, when leadership takes the time to invest in people, the culture can transform from toxic to thriving, allowing individuals to flourish in a truly supportive environment.

By the early 2000s, the Detroit Lions were wandering through their version of a desert. Much like the Israelites, they endured years of struggle—no bread, water, or hope. Their once-promising seasons had dwindled into mediocrity with no signs of improvement. The desert was a place of disillusionment and suffering, where the team, its coaches, and ownership turned on each other in frustration. The fans, too, were restless, lost in a wilderness of disappointment. Ownership failed to provide the leadership needed to guide the team, and coaching changes came and went like shifting sands, offering little more than temporary relief.

The Lions were like a nation in exile—lacking a leader who could lead them out of their misery. Their mismanagement—highlighted by poor drafts, uninspired coaching, and a workplace culture of dysfunction—kept the team trapped in a cycle of failure. Coaching changes were frequent, but none of them brought lasting success. It was as if the franchise could never find its Moses.

Then, like the Israelites, the Lions hit rock bottom. In 2008, they became the first NFL team to finish a season 0-16 (Woodyard, 2024). It was the ultimate humiliation—a time when their collective suffering felt endless. Employees within the organization described a culture of dysfunction, where accountability was scarce and communication was nonexistent. The leadership was fragmented, and hope seemed as distant as the Promised Land.

Coaching through these dark years was a grim parade of names: Marty Mornhinweg, with his 5-27 record, failed to steer the ship, while Steve Mariucci and Rod Marinelli, though experienced, were crippled by management's poor decisions. Marinelli, perhaps the most tragic figure of all, witnessed the team's historic 0-16 season, an episode so low that it seemed the Lions were stuck in an endless desert, wandering without direction. Lastly, let us not lose sight of perhaps the most feisty Lions coach, Jim Schwartz, who took the reins in 2009. Schwartz embodied the "Detroit vs. Everybody" attitude, a mindset highlighted by the infamous post-game handshake with then-San Francisco head coach Jim Harbaugh. Harbaugh's overly aggressive approach rubbed Schwartz the wrong way, leading to a heated exchange that became a symbolic moment for a team desperate for an identity. However, even Schwartz's fiery spirit could not fully overcome the organizational chaos, and once again, the Lions were left to search for answers, trapped in the same cycle of disappointment (Thomas, 2020).

However, then came a shift—a Moses-like intervention.

In the 2010s, the Lions attempted to change course, bringing in experienced leaders like Jim Caldwell and general manager Bob Quinn. Like Moses striking the stone, Caldwell managed to get the Lions to drink from the cup of respectability. Caldwell led the team to back-to-back winning seasons, including a playoff appearance in 2016, but like the Israelites, the Lions were still stuck in a cycle of disappointment. Their success was short-lived, and the internal culture remained fractured, with reports of poor leadership, lack of communication, and organizational dysfunction surfacing repeatedly.

The Lions' issues went beyond the field of play; they were about identity and internal strife. Despite Caldwell's steady hand, the organization struggled to build a supportive, healthy workplace environment. Players and staff described a culture that clung to outdated practices and was resistant to modern management strategies. Much like the Israelites in their wandering, the organization could not find its way out of its limitations.

In this context, the Lions looked for new hope in Matt Patricia, a defensive-minded coach who seemed like the answer. Much like the Israelites seeking a new path after their exodus, Patricia was supposed to be the one to lead the Lions to the Promised Land. Nevertheless, Patricia's tenure quickly became a nightmare (Shaheen, 2020). His first season started with optimism, but quickly deteriorated into another failure. By 2020, the Lions were again in the desert, their hopes dashed by another coaching misstep.

Then, amid the ruins, the Lions finally began recognizing their exodus. There was no more Moses—no single coach to solve all their problems. Instead, they needed a collective transformation. They needed to recognize that the desert was only a temporary stop. They had to leave behind their internal struggles, shed the weight of past failures, and trust that a new dawn could be on the horizon.

In 2024, with Dan Campbell at the helm, the Lions began their ascent from the wilderness. Under his leadership, they took their first steps toward healing the wounds of the past, and the team slowly found hope again. Like manna from heaven, the promise of success began to surface. The team began to eat, drink, and finally feel a sense of belonging and purpose. However, the road to redemption was much like the Israelites; the Lions' journey was not straightforward. The desert had shaped them, and only through constant struggle and growth could they finally begin to reach their potential.

As the Lions continue to rebuild, it is important to remember that this story of suffering, turning against each other, and blaming ownership and management has deep roots. Just as the Israelites' journey began long before they entered the desert, the Lions' trials began long before the 2008 disaster. There were periods of prosperity when the franchise tasted victory, such as during the championship years under George "Potsy" Clark in the 1930s or Buddy Parker in the 1950s (NFL Football Operations, n.d.). However, those years were fleeting, and the franchise found itself again in the desert, searching for a way out.

So, what is the lesson here? The Lions' suffering in the desert has been a long and complicated journey. It was never just about bad coaching or poor ownership decisions in a single decade. It culminated in years of mismanagement, misdirection, and missed opportunities. Nevertheless, just like Moses striking the stone and bringing water to the Israelites, there is always the chance for renewal for the team to break free from the desert of despair and into a future filled with hope.

It may not come overnight, but the Lions are finally coming. And this time, they will not be lost in the wilderness forever.

In 2021, the Ford family hired new Head Coach Dan Campbell, hoping to shift the team's fortunes both on and off the field. The organization appeared to be attempting a cultural overhaul, prioritizing transparency, improving player relationships, and better communication. However, this change came only after decades of issues that created a fractured relationship between the Lions and their players, staff, and fans.

While there were signs of improvement, particularly regarding team culture and communication under Campbell's leadership, the lingering effects of years of poor management, inconsistent leadership, and internal dysfunction continued to haunt the organization. The Lions' inability to maintain a consistent and positive workplace culture left a scar that would take significant time and effort to overcome.

Since 2021, the Detroit Lions have undergone a remarkable transformation that mirrors the resilience, grit, and work ethic that have long characterized the city of Detroit. This shift has been nothing short of a cultural renaissance for the franchise, driven by a leadership group that has understood one simple yet profound principle: culture eats strategy for breakfast (The Alternative Board, 2020). The Lions have cultivated a unique, thriving organizational culture by embracing values that prioritize humility, hard work, accountability, and a relentless pursuit of excellence. This culture is aligned at every level of the Detroit Lions franchise, from ownership to the players on the field. The results have been evident: for the first time in decades, the Lions have shown sustained competitiveness, promising growth, and a passionate, loyal fan base that has seen their team's potential and embraced it.

This cultural shift in Detroit's NFL franchise is deeply rooted in the long-standing values that have historically defined Detroit's industrial businesses. From General Motors to Ford, Carhartt, and American Axle, the city's most enduring corporations share common principles: hard work, humility, continuous improvement, and a commitment to doing things the right way. These principles, carried over into the football field, have transformed the Lions' on-field performance and created an environment that mirrors the best practices of Fortune 500 companies regarding leadership, employee engagement, and long-term success. This new vision focused on acquiring talent and reshaping the organization from the inside out. The result? The Lions' success in recent years, particularly in 2023 when the team made the playoffs for the first time in six years and won nine of their last eleven games, can be directly attributed to this commitment to organizational culture. This book began during the 2024 NFL season, when the Lions held the best record in the league and were pacing to contend for their first Super Bowl title.

When Sheila Hamp took over ownership in 2021, it was clear that she was determined to instill a new culture of collaboration, transparency, and long-term growth within the organization. Her leadership was informed by the work ethic and values that have long been associated with Detroit's industrial roots: a focus on building trust, being grounded, and doing things the right way—regardless of how long it might take. With the appointment of General

Manager Brad Holmes, a leader who shared her vision for a patient, long-term rebuild, and Head Coach Dan Campbell, who brought infectious energy, accountability, and grit to the sideline, the Lions began their cultural reformation.

Dan Campbell's leadership style has fostered a highly motivated, hardworking, and unified team. His emphasis on grit, humility, and accountability has become synonymous with the Lions' culture. Campbell's belief in doing things the right way—focusing on fundamentals, building relationships with players, and fostering an environment where players are challenged and supported—has laid the foundation for the Lions' resurgence. This approach mirrors the legacy of Detroit's industrial businesses that have weathered challenges by focusing on core principles and continually adapting to changing circumstances.

Brad Holmes, meanwhile, has excelled in building a sustainable, future-focused roster through the draft, emphasizing the same values of hard work, teamwork, and personal development. Like a traditional Fortune 500 company CEO, Holmes has focused on creating an environment where everyone in the organization, from the players to the front office, is aligned toward a shared vision. He recognizes that the key to success is not just about getting the right people, but getting everyone on the same page and ensuring that collaboration flows seamlessly from the top down. This alignment has resulted in a balanced, competitive team with offensive and defensive cohesion, demonstrating a deep understanding of team dynamics and a commitment to execution.

There is a striking similarity between the Detroit Lions' transformation and the principles that guide traditional Fortune 500 companies. Many successful long-standing companies—General Motors, Ford, Carhartt, American Axle, and others—are built on strong, coherent cultures that align all levels of the organization toward common goals. Whether these businesses produce cars, workwear, or automotive components, their success hinges on the ability to have every employee, from the factory floor to the executive suite, operating in sync.

What sets these businesses apart is not just their innovation or their products, but their ability to create a unified organizational culture that values integrity, collaboration, and long-term growth. When people at all levels of an organization understand their roles and share a vision of success, they work not just for their achievement, but for the collective good of the organization.

Detroit's industrial giants' strength comes from their shared commitment to values like humility, hard work, and respect for the people who do the work. Visionary leaders like Henry Ford and later corporate leaders recognized that business success was rooted in building a culture of accountability and trust, deeply embedding these values in the company's practices.

Similarly, the Detroit Lions have embraced this same approach, especially since 2021. From the leadership of Sheila Hamp to the collaborative efforts of Brad Holmes, Dan Campbell, and the assistant coaches, the Lions' culture is based on clear communication, mutual trust, and respect for all stakeholders—from players to coaches to front-office staff. This alignment has improved their performance and ability to build a sustainable, competitive team. Nevertheless, more importantly, it has allowed them to create a work environment where everyone pulls in the same direction, no matter their role.

Chapter 2: What Is Culture: The "Make-or-Break" Factor

A professional work environment culture refers to the collective values, behaviors, attitudes, and practices that define how employees interact with each other and with their organization (Fitzgerald, 2020). It shapes the day-to-day work experience, guides business operations, and influences the overall success and well-being of both employees and the organization. For Detroit Lions fans, this idea of teamwork and shared vision is something they see in their favorite team, which has embraced a culture shift in recent seasons, fostering a sense of unity. The concept of collective values and the transformation of individuals echoes the faith-based belief that when people align with shared principles, they can overcome challenges. To those critically analyzing workplace culture, the need for an environment that fosters mutual respect and a common purpose is key to long-term success, mirroring the structural changes necessary to improve team performance and organizational health.

Respect and Inclusivity: Employees treat each other with consideration, valuing different perspectives and experiences. There is an emphasis on listening, mutual respect, and maintaining a courteous, professional demeanor. In the world of sports, like the Detroit Lions, respect and inclusivity foster teamwork among diverse athletes, and a well-knit team celebrates every individual's uniqueness while working toward a common goal. This also resonates with the biblical notion that every person has inherent value, and through mutual respect and understanding, goodness can emerge from what seems to be chaos. In workplace culture, when inclusivity is at the forefront, it prevents divisions and promotes productivity—essential for personal growth and corporate success.

Clear Communication and Transparency: There is open and honest communication across all levels of the organization. Expectations, feedback, and information are shared clearly and promptly. For Lions fans, transparent communication within the team—whether between the coach and players or among the players—results in better coordination on and off the field. This aligns with Christian beliefs that transparency and truth are central to a community's strength, echoing the idea that when communication is pure and honest, it builds trust and transforms situations for the better. Workplace culture thrives when clarity is given to every employee, as it allows everyone to understand their role and contributes to achieving the organization's broader mission.

Collaboration and Teamwork: People work together to achieve common goals. Teamwork is encouraged, and cross-functional collaboration is valued. In the NFL, especially for the Detroit Lions, this type of teamwork is essential for overcoming adversity, with players like Jared Goff and Amon-Ra St. Brown illustrating how collaboration leads to wins. For those who hold Christian beliefs, the collective effort is the ultimate manifestation of faith—the idea that through unity, the team (or community) achieves greatness in God's name. From a workplace perspective, when individuals collaborate and support each other, collective energy propels the organization forward, transcending individual struggles and building a harmonious work environment.

Professionalism, Accountability, and Work Ethic: Employees maintain high work standards, focusing on efficiency, attention to detail, and meeting deadlines. In sports, the professional approach of the Lions reflects a commitment to excellence, where each player takes responsibility for their role, knowing that their contribution impacts the team's success. Christian individuals may see this principle as akin to the spiritual practice of accountability—where the individual's actions contribute to a greater purpose, transforming personal challenges into opportunities for spiritual growth. In a workplace culture context, these values are crucial to achieving organizational goals; individuals must be accountable for maintaining trust and fostering a work environment where everyone desires to give their best.

Work-Life Balance with Respect for Personal Time: A professional work environment recognizes the importance of work-life balance. The Detroit Lions' recent improvement is a testament to the importance of this balance as players manage their physical and mental health for peak performance. For Christian believers, respecting personal time aligns with the Sabbath concept, where rest is restorative and essential for maintaining a healthy mind, body, and spirit. Workplace culture flourishes when employees are encouraged to recharge, reducing burnout and increasing long-term productivity and happiness.

Growth and Development Opportunities for Learning: The organization promotes ongoing professional development, offering training, mentorship, and career advancement opportunities. Just as the Detroit Lions have invested in the growth of their young players, organizations that emphasize continuous improvement foster a culture of success. For those who celebrate Christianity, growth and transformation are key themes, much like spiritual development, where individuals can grow and evolve. In the workplace, offering growth opportunities and mentorship ensures that employees remain engaged, motivated, and loyal to the organization, resulting in sustained organizational success.

Innovation and Adaptability Encouraging Creativity: Employees are encouraged to bring new ideas and innovative solutions. For the Detroit Lions, the willingness to innovate has been a key driver of success, with new strategies allowing them to compete at higher levels. For Christians, the story of redemption mirrors this concept—where embracing new perspectives and ideas can lead to profound transformation, changing "evil" into "good." A workplace culture that values innovation encourages employees to think outside the box, driving creativity and allowing the company to adapt to a constantly changing world.

Leadership and Support: Leaders are approachable, demonstrate integrity, and lead by example. For Lions fans, leadership is embodied in figures like Dan Campbell, who inspires players by holding them accountable and showing unwavering support. Christian traditions often emphasize leadership through service, with leaders guiding by example, like Christ, whose actions teach love, sacrifice, and integrity. In a workplace culture, effective leadership fosters trust and respect, encouraging employees to reach their potential and achieve personal and organizational goals.

Trust and Integrity: Employees and leadership trust each other to act in the company's best interests and uphold professional standards. The Detroit Lions' revival is underpinned by a deep trust between management, coaching staff, and players. For Christians, trust in divine wisdom and integrity is central to faith, affirming the belief that good will eventually triumph. In the workplace, fostering trust ensures employees feel secure, empowering them to align with the company's values and mission and ensuring long-term success.

Safety and Well-Being: A professional work culture ensures that the physical and emotional workspace is safe. Just as the Detroit Lions create a secure environment for players to thrive, organizations should prioritize their teams' emotional and physical safety. For Christians, safety and well-being are deeply rooted in the idea of sanctuary—where individuals are protected, can make mistakes, and grow from them in a nurturing environment. Professional workplaces flourish when employees feel psychologically safe to express themselves, innovate, and collaborate without fear of retribution or failure.

The concept of "culture" has long been recognized as the ultimate make-or-break factor in the success of both sports teams and Fortune 500 companies. The most successful companies understand that fostering a culture that values collaboration, transparency, and long-term growth is far more important than short-term financial gains or quick fixes (Dewar). Similarly, in the NFL, organizations that build strong team cultures are the ones that thrive, even during difficult seasons. The Green Bay Packers, the New England Patriots, and the Pittsburgh Steelers all share a long-term commitment to culture—ensuring that everyone from the front office to the locker room understands their role and aligns with the organization's core values. Even though these teams have a long-standing history of success, the culture being lived out by their players on and off the field is questionable.

The Green Bay Packers are one of the most storied franchises in the NFL, with a rich history that includes multiple championships and legendary players such as Vince Lombardi, Bart Starr, and Brett Favre. However, in recent years, the franchise has faced challenges in maintaining a strong connection between the team's traditional culture and the evolving personalities of its star players. This struggle is most evident in the case of Aaron Rodgers, one of the greatest quarterbacks in the Packers' history.

Rodgers, known for his remarkable talent and football IQ, is also recognized for his distinct personality, which sometimes has clashed with the Packers' established culture. Green Bay has long been a blue-collar, hardworking, community-oriented organization. The team's culture has always been centered on a team-first mentality, humility, and modesty, traits epitomized by the Packers' past legends, including Favre. However, Rodgers, though immensely talented, has consistently shown a more individualistic approach to the game.

One of the key sources of tension between Rodgers and the Packers' culture has been his desire for control over team decisions, particularly regarding player personnel and organizational strategy. Rodgers has not shied away from publicly voicing his frustrations with the front office, notably in 2021 when he demanded a trade due to dissatisfaction with the Packers' management decisions, including the team's draft handling and roster-building. His public comments, such as expressing dissatisfaction over the Packers' failure to sign more high-profile free agents, starkly contrast the typically reserved and team-focused nature of Green Bay's public image.

His nonconformist behavior off the field has further highlighted Rodgers's desire for autonomy. He has frequently made headlines for his unorthodox views, such as his stance on COVID-19 vaccinations, which became a point of public controversy in 2021. His decisions, often seen as challenging the norms of the league and his team's expectations, have created a rift between him and the organization, which places a premium on maintaining unity and conformity to the team's broader goals. In contrast to the Packers' culture of humility and quiet professionalism, Rodgers's outspoken nature and tendency to go against the grain have sparked tension in the locker room and with fans.

This conflict between Rodgers's individuality and the Packers' traditional culture of discipline, teamwork, and community focus led to a prolonged uncertainty about his future in Green Bay. Ultimately, Rodgers's desire for more control was somewhat acknowledged, with the Packers making several moves to accommodate his demands, including restructuring his contract and providing him with a greater voice in player acquisitions. However, these compromises have not fully resolved the underlying tension between Rodgers's aspirations and the Packers' organizational culture, which continues to navigate how much influence a star player should have within a team that prides itself on collective success.

The Green Bay Packers' struggles with balancing their traditional culture with the desires of star players, a.k.a. toxic employees like Aaron Rodgers, reflect the broader challenges many NFL teams face as the league evolves. While Rodgers's talent and leadership have undeniably brought the team success, his individualism has sometimes conflicted with the Packers' ethos, resulting in a complicated and, at times, contentious relationship. The situation with Rodgers highlights the tension between maintaining a strong, cohesive team culture and adapting to the growing influence of individual players seeking more control over their careers and teams.

The New England Patriots are one of the most successful franchises in NFL history, known for their disciplined, team-oriented culture under the leadership of Head Coach Bill Belichick and the presence of star quarterback Tom Brady. The Patriots have built their identity on a "do your job" mentality, emphasizing hard work, collective effort, and unselfishness. However, even within this tightly controlled system, certain players have struggled to align with the franchise's traditional culture fully. One of the most notable examples of this conflict is the case of Wes Welker, a standout wide receiver who became one of the Patriots' most prolific players but eventually faced challenges with the organization's culture.

Welker, who joined the Patriots in 2007, quickly emerged as one of the NFL's most effective and beloved receivers, known for his quickness, precision, and ability to work the slot position. Despite his success on the field, Welker's personality and relationship with the Patriots' culture were sometimes at odds. The Patriots' system, under Belichick, values consistency, discipline, and the ability to fit into the team-first mentality. In contrast, Welker, while highly productive, was known for his outspoken and emotional nature, often expressing his frustrations more openly than many of his teammates. This occasionally put him at odds with the Patriots' typically reserved approach.

One of the primary points of tension between Welker and the Patriots was his contract situation. Throughout his time in New England, Welker frequently found himself in contract disputes, seeking better compensation to reflect his status as one of the league's top receivers. The Patriots, however, were known for their reluctance to hand out large contracts, especially to non-quarterback players, and often took a pragmatic approach to player contracts. This led to several public standoffs, including during the 2012 offseason when Welker sought a long-term contract extension. The Patriots eventually franchised him, but this decision left Welker feeling undervalued and frustrated, a sentiment that was hard to reconcile with the Patriots' emphasis on team over individual desires.

Furthermore, Welker's relationship with the team was tested during the 2013 Super Bowl when he dropped a critical pass in the game's final minutes. While Belichick and his teammates publicly supported Welker, the moment seemed to encapsulate the high-pressure nature of playing in New England. The Patriots' culture places immense importance on executing in the clutch, and mistakes, especially in the postseason, can cause friction. While Welker was undeniably a key contributor to the Patriots' offense, this moment and his subsequent departure from the team in 2013 reflected how the pressure of New England's system could wear on players who, despite being highly skilled, did not entirely mesh with the more impersonal, results-driven mentality of the organization.

Welker's departure from New England, when he signed with the Denver Broncos, was also a sign of the disconnect between the player and the organization. Although the Patriots would go on to win another Super Bowl without him, Welker's exit highlighted the difficulty some players face in living up to the team-first, "Patriot Way" culture. Unlike many star players who thrive in this system, Welker's more open demeanor and emotional approach to the game seemed to clash with the Patriots' often cold and outdated businesslike environment.

Wes Welker's time with the New England Patriots is a clear example of how even exceptional players struggle with the team's demanding culture. Despite his success, Welker's battles with contract issues, his emotional nature, and occasional mistakes created tensions with an organization built on discipline, consistency, and the suppression of individual egos. His time in New England exemplifies how a player's approach to the game can sometimes clash with a team's culture, even within an organization as successful as the Patriots.

The Pittsburgh Steelers, one of the most successful and storied franchises in NFL history, have long prided themselves on a strong team-oriented culture. Known for their "Steelers Way," the team emphasizes hard work, discipline, and a focus on collective success. Under Head Coach Mike Tomlin, the Steelers have built their identity around consistency, toughness, and a commitment to team-first principles. However, in recent years, one of the most talented players in the team's history, wide receiver Antonio Brown, has exemplified the struggles that can arise when individual desires clash with a franchise's established culture.

Antonio Brown, drafted by the Steelers in 2010, quickly became one of the NFL's most dynamic and electrifying receivers. His skills on the field, including incredible route-running, speed, and ability to make spectacular catches, made him the focal point of Pittsburgh's offense for nearly a decade. Brown's work ethic and talent were undeniable, and he broke numerous franchise records during his time with the Steelers. However, despite his success, Brown's personality and actions began to diverge from the culture that had defined the team for so long.

One of the primary tensions between Brown and the Steelers stemmed from his increasing desire for individual recognition and control. As he became one of the league's top wide receivers, Brown sought more influence over his career, particularly in a more significant contract and a more prominent role in team decisions. In 2017, he received a massive contract extension, but his desire for further recognition and financial compensation grew. Brown's behavior became egocentric, with frequent public displays of frustration over his treatment within the organization. This included a high-profile dispute with quarterback Ben Roethlisberger, whom Brown publicly criticized, and a series of social media posts showcased his growing dissatisfaction.

The Steelers' culture, rooted in discipline and teamwork, sharply contrasted with Brown's increasingly unpredictable behavior. His actions on social media, such as live-streaming a post-game locker room speech, were viewed as a clear violation of the team's established commitment to professionalism and minimizing distractions. The Steelers, who prided themselves on keeping their business out of the public eye, found themselves at odds with Brown's increasingly public and personal approach to handling conflicts.

Brown's growing sense of entitlement and refusal to adhere to the team's collective ethos peaked in 2018. After a heated dispute with Roethlisberger and being benched for the final game of the regular season due to a conflict with the coaching staff, it became clear that Brown's relationship with the team had broken down. Brown's behavior was at odds with the Steelers' team-first philosophy, prioritizing accountability and the group's well-being.

Ultimately, the tension between Brown's ambitions and the Steelers' organizational culture led to his trade to the Oakland Raiders in 2019. While Brown's talent was undeniable, his departure from Pittsburgh was emblematic of the difficulty even elite players face in maintaining alignment with a team culture that values collective achievement over individual fame. His time in Pittsburgh showed that, despite all of his accomplishments on the field, his approach to the game—one that prioritized his brand and individual desires—was incompatible with the Steelers' traditional, team-first approach.

Antonio Brown's time with the Pittsburgh Steelers highlights a team's challenges when a star player's individualism clashes with the organization's culture. Brown's immense talent and production on the field were overshadowed by his increasingly disruptive behavior and desire for personal recognition. The Steelers' commitment to teamwork, discipline, and professionalism could not withstand the tension created by Brown's growing focus on his brand, ultimately leading to his exit from the team. His story serves as a reminder of how even the most gifted athletes can struggle to fit into a team culture that places a premium on unity and collective success.

For the Detroit Lions, aligning everyone—ownership, management, coaches, and players—has been a game-changer. The team's turnaround proves that success is far more attainable when culture is prioritized and consistently nurtured. The 2021-2024 seasons have shown that the Lions' leadership is building a competitive roster and cultivating a sense of unity and purpose within the organization. Players like Jared Goff, Amon-Ra St. Brown, and Aiden Hutchinson embody the traits of hard work, humility, and resilience, and their commitment to the team's mission has created a winning mentality that extends far beyond the football field.

In the world of business, the same principle holds true. Companies that align their people—from the CEO to the newest hire—around a shared vision and values tend to have better long-term success. This alignment creates an environment where employees feel motivated, valued, and empowered to contribute to the company's success. Organizations can swiftly become disjointed without alignment as different departments operate at odds, ultimately jeopardizing the company's long-term objectives (George et al., 2021).

The Detroit Lions' organizational culture has ensured that every part of the team is working toward the same end: sustained success. By fostering an environment where trust, accountability, and commitment to doing things the right way are paramount, the Lions have set themselves up for long-term growth—just as Detroit's industrial giants have done throughout history.

The Detroit Lions' success since 2021 is not just a product of talent acquisition or strategic game plans, but of the deliberate creation of a unified, resilient culture. This culture, inspired by the values of hard work, humility, and the relentless pursuit of excellence that have defined Detroit's legacy businesses, has transformed the Lions into a competitive, well-aligned organization. The team's leadership, from Sheila Hamp and Brad Holmes to Dan Campbell and his coaching staff, has embraced the principle that culture is the ultimate make-or-break factor in sustained success.

The same principle holds for legacy companies in Detroit. General Motors, Ford, Carhartt, and American Axle have long understood that long-term success hinges on making great products and creating a work culture where everyone, at every level, is aligned toward a shared goal. When companies—like sports teams—have a unified culture where everyone is on the same page, that culture becomes the foundation for lasting success. For the Detroit Lions and the great businesses that call Detroit home, that alignment is the key to staying competitive, relevant, and resilient—no matter what challenges lie ahead.

Chapter 3: The New Gold Standard

In recent years, the Detroit Lions have emerged as one of the most surprising and impressive examples of how a professional sports organization can successfully overhaul its workplace culture, positioning itself as a leading case study in employee satisfaction, team cohesion, and organizational success. The Lions, a storied franchise in the NFL, have gone through a remarkable transformation that not only rejuvenated their on-field performance but also set new standards for workplace culture in the sports industry. Their approach is now being hailed as one of the most mind-blowing examples of how investing in culture can directly influence both employee engagement and team performance.

When we examine modern workplace culture, there are striking parallels between the values and principles that today's most successful organizations prioritize and the teachings of Jesus Christ: respect, collaboration, transparency, accountability, well-being, and empowerment. Although Jesus lived over 2,000 years ago, His message provided a revolutionary framework for creating a culture that elevates individuals, promotes unity, and leads to a greater sense of purpose. His approach transcends religious context and offers timeless insights into building a healthy, thriving environment—be it a community, workplace, or team. Whether or not the Detroit Lions organization realizes this, here's a closer look at how the Lions have achieved such extraordinary success by focusing on a culture centered on Christian teachings:

1. Commitment to Inclusion and Empowerment

The Lions have gone beyond the conventional corporate diversity initiatives by embedding inclusivity as a core value within the team. They made intentional efforts to diversify their front office, coaching staff, and player roster, creating an environment where every voice is heard. From hiring practices to team-building exercises, the Lions have worked hard to ensure that employees—whether coaches, players, or staff—feel like they belong.

This commitment to inclusivity and empowerment mirrors the biblical teaching of the body of Christ in 1 Corinthians 12:12-27. Paul writes that the church is like a body with many parts, each having a unique role but equally important. Just as the Lions emphasize that each person, regardless of their background or position, has a vital contribution to make, Christians are taught that every member of the church, regardless of their status or gifts, plays a role in God's greater mission. The principle of empowering and valuing every individual aligns with the teachings of unity and mutual respect in Christ, where everyone is seen as equally important in God's kingdom. Just as the Detroit Lions, for example, emphasize inclusivity by promoting diverse voices in leadership, today's organizations thrive when they create cultures that value every individual, regardless of background, role, or status. Companies that truly embrace diversity and respect the uniqueness of every employee cultivate a sense of belonging that fuels engagement and creativity (Join The Collective, 2024).

2. Employee Engagement and Team Collaboration

The Lions have implemented a culture of open communication across every department—coaching, marketing, operations, and more—allowing for better collaboration and innovation. Employees at all levels are encouraged to voice their ideas and concerns. This collaborative environment has directly translated into more efficient decision-making and better overall team performance. The franchise has invested in employee recognition programs that highlight both on-field and off-field successes. The Lions celebrate milestones, not just for players, but for all staff members, ensuring that their contributions are seen and appreciated, fostering a sense of shared purpose.

This collaborative approach is akin to the biblical teaching of unity and working together for a common purpose found in Philippians 2:1-4. Paul encourages the church to "be of the same mind, having the same love, being in full accord and of one mind." Just as the Lions prioritize collaboration to strengthen the team, Christians are called to work in unity, encouraging each other and sharing in the mission of advancing God's kingdom. The Christian concept of servant leadership (Mark 10:42-45), where leaders are expected to serve rather than dominate, parallels the Lions' approach to acknowledging every team member's contribution. In Matthew 20:26-28, Jesus introduces the concept of "servant leadership," telling his disciples: "Whoever wants to become great among you must be your servant, and whoever wants to be first must be your slave." This radical idea turned the traditional power structures of the time upside down. Instead of lording authority over others, Jesus taught that true leadership is about serving others, empowering them, and leading by example.

Today's best leaders understand that leadership is not about power, but about enabling others to succeed. The most effective leaders, like Coach Dan Campbell of the Detroit Lions, take a coaching and mentoring approach, empowering their teams through support and guidance and by creating an environment where everyone can thrive. When employees feel supported, valued, and trusted, they are more engaged, motivated, and productive.

3. Well-Being and Work-Life Balance

Recognizing the high-pressure nature of both football and sports management, the Lions have taken groundbreaking steps to prioritize mental health and emotional well-being. They have integrated mental health resources into their staff and player development programs, providing robust support systems, including regular mental wellness check-ins, counseling, and access to stress management techniques. Understanding that work-life balance extends beyond the football field, the Lions have implemented flexible working arrangements for their staff, creating a culture where people can balance their professional and personal lives more effectively. This forward-thinking approach is something that has gained them high marks from employees, with many citing it as one of the reasons they feel valued and supported.

The Lions' approach to prioritizing well-being can be compared to the biblical principle of rest and renewal. In Matthew 11:28-30, Jesus invites those who are weary and burdened to come to Him for rest. This is consistent with the Christian concept of Sabbath rest (Exodus 20:8-10), where God commands His people to rest and recharge, acknowledging that humans need rest as part of God's design. The Lions' emphasis on mental health and balance mirrors how God cares for the holistic well-being of His people, encouraging not only physical and emotional rest but also spiritual renewal. Jesus cared deeply for the well-being of His followers, emphasizing the importance of rest, renewal, and inner peace. In Matthew 11:28-30, He offers comfort and rest to the weary: "Come to me, all you who are weary and burdened, and I will give you rest. Take my yoke upon you and learn from me, for I am gentle and humble in heart, and you will find rest for your souls." He recognized the need for both spiritual and physical rest and healing.

Organizations today, like the Detroit Lions, are increasingly aware of the importance of mental health and work-life balance. Teams that offer support for well-being—whether through flexible schedules, mental health resources, or team-building activities—see higher job satisfaction and greater productivity (Fox et al., 2021). Just as Jesus cared for the holistic well-being of his followers, modern companies that invest in the overall health of their employees create a more loyal and engaged workforce.

4. Transparency and Open Communication

Under the ownership of Sheila Hamp and the leadership of GM Brad Holmes and Head Coach Dan Campbell, the Lions have embraced a transparent, open approach to leadership. They consistently communicate their vision for the team and the organization, ensuring that everyone is aligned on goals, strategies, and expectations. Employees and players alike report feeling that they are a part of something bigger, understanding not just their individual roles but the broader mission of the team. Employee feedback is not only welcomed but actively sought after. The Lions collect feedback from players through a combination of player meetings, individual coach-player conversations, anonymous surveys, post-game reviews, and a dedicated feedback platform where players can submit their thoughts and concerns directly to the coaching staff at any time. This feedback has driven many changes in how the team operates, showing a commitment to continuous improvement.

This mirrors the biblical idea of truth and honesty in relationships, as seen in Ephesians 4:15-16, where Paul encourages the church to speak the truth in love, building one another up. In a similar way, the Lions' transparent communication cultivates trust and alignment within the team. Christians are called to operate with honesty and transparency, ensuring that all members of the body understand and contribute to God's purposes. Open communication in the workplace reflects the biblical call to mutual accountability (James 5:16), where each person is encouraged to speak the truth in love and grow together in unity. Jesus was known for speaking the truth boldly and transparently, regardless of the consequences. In Matthew 5:37, He instructs: "Let your 'Yes' be 'Yes,' and your 'No,' 'No.' Anything beyond this comes from the evil one." His honesty and directness, combined with His willingness to hold His followers accountable, laid the foundation for a culture based on integrity and authenticity.

Transparency in leadership and clear communication are crucial in any high-functioning organization. Just as the Detroit Lions embrace transparency through open communication about their goals and performance, organizations thrive when employees understand the direction the company is heading and feel accountable for contributing to that vision. This honesty fosters trust, engagement, and commitment among teams.

5. Innovation, Adaptability, and Forgiveness

The Detroit Lions are leveraging cutting-edge technologies like performance tracking, Virtual Reality, and Augmented Reality to enhance player training and strategy (Brighton, 2024). These tools provide real-time insights into player health and game strategy, helping improve performance and decision-making. While these innovations offer benefits like better training, injury prevention, and increased engagement, they also come with challenges, such as high costs and a learning curve. As the Lions lead the way in tech adoption, other NFL teams are likely to follow, making these methods more common in the league. From state-of-the-art facilities to cutting-edge performance tracking software, the team has equipped their employees with the tools they need to succeed in an increasingly digital world. This focus on innovation has been particularly crucial in adapting to changing dynamics in sports, ensuring that the Lions remain competitive not just on the field, but in every aspect of the organization. Coach Dan Campbell's leadership style has been a game-changer. Known for his authentic, empathetic approach to coaching, Campbell has cultivated a culture where adaptability and growth are not just encouraged but expected. His leadership has helped the Lions transition from a team with a history of underperformance to a young, hungry squad that's become a rising force in the NFL.

The principle of innovation and adaptability aligns with the biblical concept of growth and transformation (Romans 12:2), where believers are encouraged to be transformed by the renewing of their minds. Just as the Lions embrace innovation to stay competitive, Christians are called to adapt to God's changing call on their lives, growing in wisdom and knowledge. The adaptability of the Lions is also akin to the apostle Paul's message in 1 Corinthians 9:22, where he says, "I have become all things to all people so that by all possible means I might save some." This passage illustrates the importance of being adaptable to effectively carry out one's mission, a principle that is equally valuable in both sports and faith. In addition, Jesus consistently taught the importance of forgiveness and reconciliation. In Matthew 18:21-22, when Peter asks how many times one should forgive, Jesus responds: "I tell you, not seven times, but seventy-seven times." This radical call to forgive emphasizes the importance of healing relationships and maintaining harmony within communities.

In the workplace, conflict is inevitable, but how it is handled defines the overall culture. Companies with a strong culture encourage resolution through understanding, forgiveness, and constructive feedback. The Detroit Lions, for example, have cultivated a culture of growth and accountability, where mistakes are opportunities for learning rather than blame. By fostering an environment of forgiveness and conflict resolution, teams can move forward stronger and more united.

6. Recognition and Awards for Culture

As a direct result of its cultural transformation, the Detroit Lions have received numerous accolades for being one of the top organizations to work for in the sports industry. Their efforts have been recognized not just by internal stakeholders but by industry bodies and publications that highlight the franchise as a leader in employee satisfaction and organizational development. The Lions have reported one of the highest employee retention rates in the NFL, a testament to how their work culture has created a positive environment where people want to stay (Gregory, 2024). By providing opportunities for growth, investing in team bonding, and maintaining a focus on personal well-being, the Lions have cultivated a loyal, motivated workforce.

The Lions' recognition culture reflects the Christian call to honor and encourage each other. Just as the team celebrates successes, Christians are encouraged to honor those who labor for God's kingdom. This aligns with the idea that God sees and rewards those who faithfully serve, even in humble or unseen ways (Hebrews 6:10).

7. Tangible Business Impact

As a result of these cultural investments, the Lions have seen a tangible improvement in team performance, which has been reflected in more competitive seasons and a growing fanbase. The organization's culture of accountability, inclusivity, and collaboration has translated into improved on-field results, culminating in a team that is not only better equipped to compete but also better positioned to build a sustainable championship-caliber squad. Beyond football, the Lions' cultural transformation has fueled business growth. Their focus on inclusivity, well-being, and collaboration has enhanced their brand image, attracted new sponsorships, and strengthened relationships with the Detroit community. The Lions are now seen as an integral part of the community, contributing to local initiatives and strengthening ties with fans through authentic engagement.

The Lions' focus on collaboration, transparency, and inclusion is similar to how Christians are called to bear good fruit by living in alignment with God's purposes. When organizations or individuals work with integrity, transparency, and unity, they see positive outcomes. The parable of the talents (Matthew 25:14-30) teaches that investing in what God has entrusted to us leads to multiplication and growth. This principle applies both to personal and organizational success when founded on collaboration and shared goals.

The Detroit Lions have shown the sports world—and beyond—that a strong, positive workplace culture can drive both employee satisfaction and on-field success. By focusing on inclusivity, mental health, transparency, and collaboration, the Lions have transformed themselves from a franchise often seen as a perennial underperformer to a team widely recognized for its innovative, people-first approach. The franchise is now a case study of how culture can influence everything from employee retention to performance on the field and business growth, setting a new benchmark for how NFL teams (and any organization) can leverage culture to achieve long-term success.

By tying these principles from the Detroit Lions' organizational culture to biblical teachings, we see how both the world of sports and the teachings of Christianity align in promoting values such as collaboration, empowerment, transparency, and growth. The Lions' success story can serve as a modern-day example of how these timeless principles are not only effective in achieving success but also in fostering a thriving, values-driven culture. The timeless culture of Christ's teachings provides a blueprint for an ideal workplace culture that is still relevant today. His emphasis on inclusivity, servant leadership, community, honesty, well-being, forgiveness, and purpose has profound implications for organizations seeking to build a thriving culture. Much like the modern organizations that recognize the importance of culture in driving performance and employee satisfaction, Jesus modeled a way of living that prioritizes people, unity, and collective growth—values that are foundational to any organization striving for long-term success. His model shows us that, when applied with sincerity and dedication, such a culture can indeed change the world—just as it changed the lives of those who followed Him 2,000 years ago.

Chapter 4: The Leaders

A cultural transformation to the magnitude of the Detroit Lions does not happen by chance. It requires a maniacal approach where everyone is bought in and believes in not only the mission but also the effort required along the way during the journey. Three key individuals laid the foundation for the Detroit Lions:

Dan Campbell: Head Coach

Dan Campbell has become one of the most beloved and respected leaders in the NFL, inspiring, unifying, and transforming. Known for his fiery passion, relentless work ethic, and unmatched authenticity, Campbell has quickly transformed the Lions' culture into one defined by grit, accountability, and a shared sense of purpose. Since taking over as head coach in 2021, Campbell's leadership has revitalized the team's performance and fostered an organizational culture that thrives on unity, trust, and relentless determination.

Dan Campbell's journey to becoming the head coach of the Detroit Lions is rooted in his experiences as a player and his gradual ascent through the coaching ranks. Campbell grew up in Texas, where football is more than just a sport—it is a way of life. After playing college football at Texas A&M, Campbell was fortunate to be drafted into the NFL, where he enjoyed a successful playing career as a tight end. His time in the NFL included stints with the New York Giants, Dallas Cowboys, Detroit Lions and New Orleans Saints, where he earned a reputation as a fierce competitor and a tenacious leader in the locker room.

After retiring as a player, Campbell transitioned into coaching, first serving as an assistant coach for the Miami Dolphins and later as the interim head coach in 2015. He then served as the tight ends coach and assistant head coach for the New Orleans Saints under Sean Payton. Throughout his playing and coaching career, Campbell developed a unique perspective on leadership—one that combines a deep understanding of the game with a relentless commitment to motivating, mentoring, and supporting those around him.

Intensity, authenticity, and emotional intelligence define Dan Campbell's leadership. His approach to coaching the Lions is not just about Xs and Os but about building a culture where people are empowered to be their best—on and off the field. Campbell's leadership is rooted in genuine personal connections, a clear vision, and a commitment to pushing his players and staff to their limits while always keeping them accountable and motivated.

Authenticity and Relatability: One of Campbell's defining traits is his authenticity. He is not one to put on a facade or try to be someone he is not. When he stepped into the head coach role, Campbell made it clear that he would be himself—and that was exactly what the Lions needed. His unfiltered approach, self-deprecating humor, and genuine care for people have made him an approachable and respected figure within the organization. Campbell's transparency and honesty foster trust and make it clear to players and staff that he is invested in them as individuals, not just as football players.

Emotional Intelligence and Empathy: Campbell's emotional intelligence is one of the cornerstones of his leadership style (Keefer, 2025). He understands that being a successful coach is not just about calling plays; it is about connecting with players personally and understanding their motivations, fears, and goals. His ability to read the room, provide support when needed, and challenge players to dig deeper has helped him create a team culture where everyone feels valued. Whether supporting a player through personal difficulties or helping them overcome mental and physical barriers on the field, Campbell has shown a deep level of empathy that has earned him the loyalty of his players.

Inspiring Passion and Belief: Perhaps no trait is more associated with Dan Campbell than his boundless energy and passion for the game. His speeches and press conferences have become legendary for their intensity, passion, and unapologetic love for the sport. Campbell's enthusiasm is contagious from his famous "bite a kneecap off" speech to his rallying cries in the locker room. He can inspire belief in his players—sometimes even when the odds are stacked against them. Campbell does not just want his players to perform; he wants them to believe in the team, the process, and themselves. His passion fuels the Lions' locker room, making every player feel part of something bigger than a football team.

Accountability and Tough Love: While Campbell is a coach who cares deeply for his players, he is equally committed to holding them accountable. He demands excellence in practice and games and is unafraid to push his players to their limits. Campbell believes that growth comes from discomfort and challenge and is not afraid to deliver tough love when necessary. This approach has helped shape a culture of accountability, where players know they will be held to the highest standards but also that they will receive the support they need to meet those standards. Campbell's ability to balance tough love with genuine care for his players has been key to his success as a coach.

Building a Family Culture: One of the defining elements of Campbell's leadership is the sense of family he fosters within the Lions organization. He firmly believes that the strongest teams are built on strong relationships and prioritizes developing close-knit bonds within the locker room (Woodyard, 2024). Campbell often talks about the importance of players caring for one another and having each other's backs—both on and off the field. This emphasis on camaraderie has led to a culture where the players view each other as brothers, creating a unified and highly motivated team. This family-oriented culture extends beyond the locker room, as Campbell encourages players to spend time together outside of football and to support each other in all aspects of life.

Resilience and a Growth Mindset: Campbell's leadership is also characterized by resilience—the ability to remain focused and positive when facing adversity. As a player and coach, Campbell has faced setbacks and challenges throughout his career but has always found ways to bounce back stronger. This mindset has been contagious within the Lions organization, where players are encouraged to embrace failure as a learning opportunity rather than as a setback. Campbell has instilled a growth mindset in the team, where every mistake is an opportunity to improve. This resilience and constant improvement culture has been essential in the team's transformation from a rebuilding franchise to one that competes with the best.

Leadership by Example: Campbell leads by example—his work ethic, commitment, and drive are unmatched. He is always the first in the office and the last to leave. His willingness to put in the hours, study the game, and prepare for every opponent is an example to his players and staff of what it takes to succeed at the highest level. Whether participating in drills, studying film, or helping with player development, Campbell's hands-on approach demonstrates his dedication to the team's success and sets a standard for everyone. His example of hard work and dedication has been key to creating a culture of discipline and commitment within the Lions.

Dan Campbell has worked tirelessly to create an unmatched work culture within the Detroit Lions that values performance, character, relationships, and personal growth. His leadership is about more than just winning games; it is about building a foundation for sustained success and creating an environment where everyone feels empowered to contribute.

Unity and Teamwork: Campbell's focus on building unity within the team has created a cohesive locker room where players always look out for one another. His emphasis on collaboration has extended beyond the field, where staff, coaches, and players work together toward a shared goal. Regardless of their role, everyone is vital to the team's success.

Player Development: Under Campbell's leadership, player development has become a central focus. He ensures that every player—whether a rookie or veteran—has the tools, resources, and support they need to improve. This commitment to development has helped individual players reach their full potential and contributed to the Lions' overall success on the field.

Positive, High-Energy Environment: Campbell's infectious energy creates a high-octane, positive work environment where players and staff are motivated to bring their best daily. His high standards and ability to inspire create a work culture where excellence is expected and celebrated.

Mental and Emotional Resilience: Campbell's philosophy centers on mental toughness and resilience. He encourages players to embrace adversity and never back down from a challenge. This mindset has helped transform the Lions into a team that fights through every game, regardless of the circumstances.

Dan Campbell's leadership has been a game-changer for the Detroit Lions, both on and off the field. His ability to combine passion, authenticity, emotional intelligence, and accountability has created a culture of collaboration, growth, and relentless pursuit of excellence. Campbell is not just a coach but a leader who inspires, unites, and transforms everyone he touches. Through his leadership, the Lions have developed an unmatched work culture—one poised for sustained success and built on a foundation of trust, family, and commitment to constant improvement.

Brad Holmes: General Manager

Brad Holmes quickly emerges as one of the NFL's most respected and innovative executive front-office leaders. He has built a winning culture through strategic leadership and authenticity. Since taking over as GM in 2021, Holmes has brought a fresh, forward-thinking approach to team building, marked by a genuine commitment to cultivating a positive and inclusive work culture. His leadership is defined not only by his impressive football acumen and strategic vision but also by his authentic, people-first mentality. These qualities have helped foster an organizational culture within the Lions that is collaborative, empowering, and centered on long-term growth.

Brad Holmes's upbringing and diverse professional experiences shaped the Detroit Lions General Manager. Growing up in a football-focused setting, Holmes was naturally captivated by the game from a young age. He played college football at the University of North Carolina and later earned a degree in communications. However, he could analyze and evaluate the talent that led to his career in the NFL front office.

Holmes's professional journey began with the Los Angeles Rams, where he spent eighteen years, rising through the ranks from an intern to Director of College Scouting. In his role with the Rams, he helped build one of the league's most successful rosters, playing a critical part in key draft picks and player acquisitions. Holmes's extensive scouting background and his grasp of organizational dynamics made him the perfect choice to helm the Lions as they embarked on a new era.

Brad Holmes's leadership style is rooted in his authenticity, humility, and high emotional intelligence. He is not the type of GM who seeks the spotlight; instead, he focuses on empowering those around him and fostering a culture of collaboration. His leadership has reshaped the Detroit Lions' front office, making it one of the most respected in the NFL for its emphasis on trust, accountability, and continuous improvement.

Integrity: Brad Holmes is widely recognized for his authenticity—he presents himself precisely as he is. This transparency has resonated throughout the organization, where players, coaches, and staff appreciate his straightforward communication style. Holmes is a leader who values honesty and integrity above all else. He consistently clarifies decision-making, and his actions align with his words. This authenticity has earned him the trust of everyone within the organization and allowed the Lions' front office to work cohesively with a shared purpose.

Emotional Awareness and Compassion: One of Holmes's most remarkable traits is his emotional intelligence. As a leader, he is attuned to the needs of the people around him, understanding that success in the NFL is not just about talent but about nurturing relationships and fostering a positive environment. Holmes has been described as a "player's GM" because of his empathetic approach to players and staff. He listens closely to their concerns, provides support when needed, and makes decisions prioritizing their well-being, creating loyalty and respect throughout the organization.

Strategic Vision with a Focus on Culture: Holmes possesses a rare combination of strategic foresight and a deep understanding of team dynamics. As GM, he has transformed the Lions' roster with a keen eye for talent and a long-term vision for success. However, his approach goes beyond player evaluation. He is committed to creating a winning culture that ensures lasting success for years to come. Holmes emphasizes a holistic approach to team building, where strong leadership, chemistry, and shared values are just as important as raw athletic talent. He has instilled a culture of growth and accountability, ensuring everyone—from the front office to the locker room—shares in the collective mission of rebuilding the team and achieving lasting success.

Collaboration and Empowerment: Holmes has created a work culture prioritizing collaboration and shared responsibility. Unlike some front offices that can become siloed or hierarchical, the Lions under Holmes are known for their openness and teamwork. He encourages input from his entire staff, from scouts to coaches to analysts, and ensures everyone has a voice in decision-making. This approach fosters a strong sense of ownership among all employees and creates a work environment where individuals feel empowered to contribute to the team's success. Holmes firmly believes that collaboration, rather than individualism, is the key to building something sustainable and unique.

Patience and Long-Term Thinking: In a time when quick fixes and instant success are the norm, Holmes has opted for a long-term strategy in rebuilding the Lions. He is not looking for short-term glory, but sustainable success that can carry the team into the future. His ability to stay calm and focused in the face of challenges has instilled confidence in the Lions' ownership and coaching staff. Holmes understands that turning around a franchise takes time and is committed to doing it right, one step at a time. This patient, process-driven approach has been critical in laying the foundation for a franchise that can compete for years to come.

Commitment to Diversity and Inclusion: As a leader in the NFL, Brad Holmes has made it a point to ensure that the Lions' front office is diverse, equitable, and inclusive to find players that mesh with their culture (Raven, 2022). He is a staunch advocate for diversity in the players and the organizational structure. Holmes is committed to creating opportunities for people of all backgrounds and fostering an environment where everyone, regardless of race, gender, or experience, has the chance to thrive. His focus on inclusion is also evident in his hiring practices, where he prioritizes hiring diverse staff members who bring varied perspectives to the decision-making process.

Brad Holmes has been instrumental in creating a work culture within the Detroit Lions that is unlike any other in the NFL. His ability to build relationships, focus on the well-being of his staff, and set clear expectations has led to a high-performing and cohesive environment that draws talent and promotes personal growth.

Empowering Leadership: Holmes has empowered those around him to grow and excel in their roles, whether in the front office or on the field. He trusts his team and encourages individuals to take ownership of their responsibilities. By creating a culture where everyone feels valued, Holmes has established an atmosphere where people are excited to contribute their best work.

Mentorship and Development: Holmes is deeply invested in developing his team, not just in terms of football skills but also as individuals. His mentorship goes beyond professional development; he focuses on the personal growth of the people he works with, helping them cultivate the skills they need to succeed inside and outside the NFL. This approach has led to increased retention rates and strong internal loyalty.

Employee and Player Wellness: Holmes has prioritized player and staff wellness as part of his commitment to a positive work culture. He ensures that resources are in place to support the team's mental and physical health. By prioritizing wellness, Holmes has created an environment where people feel supported, allowing them to perform at their highest level without fear of burnout.

Building Trust Through Accountability: One of Holmes's leadership hallmarks is his commitment to accountability. He expects high standards from everyone and holds himself to the same standards. His approach fosters trust; everyone knows they are part of a system where integrity and responsibility are paramount.

Brad Holmes has transformed the Detroit Lions' front office with a leadership style grounded in authenticity, emotional intelligence, and long-term vision. His commitment to creating a work culture based on collaboration, trust, and accountability has fostered a cohesive, positive environment that attracts and retains top talent. Whether it is his strategic approach to roster-building, his focus on diversity and inclusion, or his unwavering commitment to the well-being of his staff and players, Holmes's leadership is redefining what it means to be a successful GM in the modern NFL.

Under Brad Holmes's guidance, the Lions are not just building a competitive football team but cultivating a sustainable, winning culture that will endure for years. His leadership is a testament to the power of authenticity, empathy, and long-term thinking in creating an organization where people and performance can thrive.

Sheila Hamp: Owner

Sheila Hamp is a trailblazer in the world of sports leadership, known not just for her stewardship of the Detroit Lions but also for her deep commitment to creating an empowering and inclusive work culture that has reshaped the organization. As the principal owner and chairwoman of the Detroit Lions, Sheila's leadership style combines compassion, innovation, and a relentless pursuit of excellence—qualities that have earned her the respect of her peers, players, and staff.

Sheila Hamp was born into one of the most storied families in American sports. As the granddaughter of the late William Clay Ford Sr. and the daughter of the late William Clay Ford Jr., Sheila grew up deeply immersed in professional sports. However, her path to ownership was not merely a product of family inheritance; she developed her strong sense of purpose and leadership through education and personal experience. A graduate of the University of

Pennsylvania, Sheila earned her master's degree in business administration from Harvard Business School.

Before taking the helm of the Detroit Lions on June 23, 2020, Sheila built a successful career outside of sports, gaining valuable experience in various leadership roles within the Ford Motor Company and serving on the boards of several nonprofit organizations (Birkett, 2021). This professional background shaped her approach to leadership, which is grounded in analytical thinking, strategic planning, and an understanding of the importance of diverse perspectives.

Sheila Hamp's leadership style blends empathy and a strong focus on achieving results. She uniquely balances the financial and competitive demands of running a professional sports team with a deep commitment to the well-being and development of her staff, players, and community.

Empathy and Emotional Intelligence: Sheila is widely regarded for her emotional intelligence. She understands the power of human connection and has worked to foster a culture where employees feel heard and valued. In an industry often focused on performance metrics, Sheila places a premium on the mental and emotional health of the people who make up the Lions organization (Payton). Her approach has made her an approachable figure, and players, coaches, and staff frequently acknowledge her for creating an environment where open communication is encouraged.

Visionary Leadership with a Long-Term Focus: One of Sheila's most remarkable qualities is her long-term vision for the Detroit Lions. She has steadfastly committed to building a competitive football team and ensuring the organization is rooted in a sustainable and forward-thinking business model. Sheila understands that success is not just about the here and now, but about creating an enduring legacy for the franchise. She has been instrumental in ensuring that the Lions invest in facilities, player development, and technology to keep pace with the ever-evolving demands of the NFL. Under her leadership, the Lions have prioritized scouting and developing talent on and off the field, ensuring that future generations are well-prepared to succeed.

Commitment to Diversity and Inclusion: As a female owner in a male-dominated industry, Sheila has prioritized promoting diversity, equity, and inclusion throughout the Detroit Lions organization. Her leadership reflects a commitment to breaking down barriers and creating a more diverse workplace in terms of gender and ethnicity. Sheila has been outspoken in her desire to see more women in leadership roles across the NFL, and she has fostered an environment where different perspectives are not only welcomed but actively sought out.

Collaboration and Teamwork: Sheila's leadership is deeply collaborative. She values the contributions of everyone in the organization, from front-office executives to coaches to support staff. She is known for creating a sense of unity within the franchise, emphasizing the importance of teamwork both on and off the field. Her leadership style encourages a "we" over "me" mentality, which has been instrumental in creating an environment where everyone works toward a shared goal.

Commitment to Community: Sheila's work ethic and leadership extend beyond the Lions organization. She is a passionate advocate for the city of Detroit, recognizing the franchise's role in the community and the social responsibilities that come with it. Under her guidance, the Lions have increased their engagement with local communities with programs that promote youth football, education, and health initiatives. Sheila has also worked to strengthen the relationship between the Lions and Detroit's most underserved populations, reinforcing that the team is not just a business but a force for positive change in the region.

Transparency and Accountability: A key component of Sheila's leadership is her belief in transparency. While maintaining a strong sense of privacy regarding certain business matters, she is open and honest about the organization's challenges. She has built a culture of accountability within the team, where everyone—from coaches to executives—takes ownership of their actions and responsibilities. This has been particularly evident in how the Lions approach rebuilding. Sheila has been candid about the need for growth and patience, and she has empowered her leadership team to make decisions that will benefit the franchise's long-term success.

One of Sheila Hamp's most notable achievements has been her ability to create a work culture within the Detroit Lions that is unmatched in the NFL.

Employee Development: Sheila has invested heavily in the professional growth of her staff, ensuring that the people who make the Lions organization what it is have access to continuous learning opportunities. Through mentorship programs, leadership training, and professional development resources, Sheila has fostered an environment where people can thrive and reach their full potential.

Player-Centric Approach: Sheila's leadership has strongly emphasized creating a player-centric culture, focusing on helping players grow as athletes and individuals. She has supported mental health initiatives, personal development programs, and resources to help players transition to life after football. Sheila's care for her players is evident in her consistent advocacy for their well-being, reinforcing that the Detroit Lions are a family-first organization.

Employee Well-Being: Focusing on work-life balance and emotional well-being is a key tenet of Sheila's leadership. Her efforts to make the Lions a safe and supportive staff environment have increased employee satisfaction and retention. Employees regularly speak about the pride and loyalty they feel working for the organization. Sheila's leadership has created a sense of purpose beyond just the game of football.

Sheila Hamp's tenure as the principal owner of the Detroit Lions is marked by a leadership style that combines emotional intelligence, vision, and inclusivity. Her genuine care for the people within her organization and her commitment to building a culture of transparency, accountability, and community have redefined what it means to be a sports leader. Sheila's leadership has transformed the Lions' work culture and positioned the team for sustained success both on the field and in the broader community.

Under her guidance, the Detroit Lions are more than just a football team—they are a beacon of how compassionate, forward-thinking leadership can foster an environment where people are inspired to do their best work. Sheila Hamp's legacy as a transformative leader is still unfolding, and her impact will be felt for generations.

The Detroit Lions' coaching staff, led by Head Coach Dan Campbell and General Manager Brad Holmes, has created one of the NFL's most respected and cohesive coaching units. Under the leadership of Dan Campbell, the position and assistant coaches have fostered a culture built on accountability, trust, player development, and a shared commitment to excellence. Together, they form a tight-knit team where each coach brings a unique perspective and set of skills that complement one another, making the Lions' organization a model for success in both football and work culture.

These coaches are not just leaders of their position groups—they are mentors, teachers, and role models who prioritize growth, positivity, and collaboration. Whether working directly with players on the field or leading behind the scenes in meetings and preparation, this staff's collective energy, focus, and ethos have created an environment where everyone feels valued, empowered, and motivated to perform at their highest level. The Lions' coaching staff is a group that embodies the principles of hard work, accountability, and emotional intelligence, and their leadership style has been key to transforming the Lions into a competitive, resilient, and thriving team.

Assistant Head Coach Scottie Montgomery was asked on December 20, 2024, "How does the team embody the leadership of Dan Campbell?"

Montgomery: "Man, he could tell them anything. And the reason why he can tell them anything is because everything that he tells them, he believes and it is true. He is going to do it. We go out and execute a plan. It's not something that we're getting out on the field and doing on the field. It's not a 'gut' decision. We talk about these situations throughout the week. So what that looks like is a complete investment through everybody. Once you give someone a certain level of value to where you can be transparent with them? And they know what's going on? The buy-in happens. A lot of times people don't buy in because there's no investment from the person that's trying to get the buy-in and to understand what's going on. It's just 'do as I say, do what I say.' That's not how it works here. Everything is planned. Our guys understand our plan on Wednesday. They understand what we're going to do on Thursday. They understand our Friday red-zone plan and what our mentality is. So when it comes up in the game, there's no question what we're doing.

"So you're talking about buying in, yeah. He tells them it's going to be a physical week, it's going to be a physical week. They expect it. They understand it. So when he tells them, they believe it. And as a player, that's all you really want. You want somebody that can get you better. Cut all the other stuff out. Coach to player and player to coach, at the end of the day, it is 'Can you get me better?' And his track record has shown—even before he got here—that he got players better. He gets guys better. Rookies, he knows how to push their buttons. Vets, he knows how to push their buttons. And it's not 'pushing buttons' from being critical or being demeaning. He's demanding, there's no doubt. But he just knows what to do to get them over the hump" (Dunne, 2024).

While each position coach and assistant coach brings their own unique leadership style, several common themes tie them together. They are all deeply committed to creating a positive, open, and dynamic work culture that promotes growth, transparency, and mutual respect. Their leadership approaches foster environments where players and staff feel supported in their pursuit of excellence.

Collaboration and Open Communication: One of the defining characteristics of the Lions' coaching staff is their emphasis on collaboration. From the top down, the staff works in tandem, valuing open communication and collective problem-solving. Coaches are encouraged to share ideas, challenge one another, and collaborate on game plans. This mindset is reflected in how the position coaches interact with each other and their players. The Lions' staff understands that football is a team game, and they work together to create a unified strategy that aligns with the players' strengths. The position coaches foster an atmosphere where feedback and continuous learning are welcomed. Their open-door policy ensures players feel heard, valued, and comfortable approaching their coaches for guidance and support.

Player Development as the Core Focus: All Lions' position coaches share a deep passion for player development. Their approach goes beyond simply teaching skills and techniques; they are dedicated to developing the whole player as an athlete and an individual. Each coach prioritizes helping their players reach their full potential, often tailoring their coaching styles to each individual's unique needs and personalities. The staff focuses on continuous improvement and skill refinement, improving a quarterback's mechanics, a defensive lineman's pass-rush technique, or a wide receiver's route-running. This focus on player development fosters a culture of growth. Players are not afraid to make mistakes because they know that the coaching staff will help them learn from those experiences. The result is an environment where players are not just becoming better football players but better teammates, leaders, and individuals.

Trust and Accountability: The Lions' coaching staff operates on mutual trust. Coaches trust their players to execute the game plan, and players trust their coaches to provide the tools and guidance they need to succeed. This reciprocal trust is integral to the team's success. However, trust is never taken for granted—it is built through consistent performance and accountability. Coaches hold their players to high standards and emphasize the importance of responsibility, both on and off the field. Every coach instills that individual success is tied to collective success, and each player is accountable for their role in the system. This creates a team culture where everyone is motivated to give their best and support one another in achieving their goals.

Positive Reinforcement and Empowerment: While the coaches of the Detroit Lions hold their players accountable, they also know the value of positive reinforcement. Each coach makes an effort to celebrate individual and team successes, whether it is a well-executed play or an improvement in a player's performance. This positive reinforcement is not just about praising results; it is about recognizing the effort and growth that players demonstrate over time. Coaches empower their players by giving them the confidence and tools to make decisions on the field and take ownership of their development. This creates an atmosphere where players feel trusted, capable, and inspired to push themselves beyond their limits.

Humility and Continuous Learning: One of the standout qualities of the Lions' position coaches is their humility. Despite their success and expertise, these coaches understand there is always room to learn and grow. This humility is evident in their willingness to listen to feedback, learn from their players, and continuously evolve as coaches. They are open to new ideas and are not afraid to adjust their approach if it benefits the team. This continuous improvement mindset permeates the entire organization and is passed down to the players, creating a culture of lifelong learning and adaptability.

Supportive Leadership with a Focus on Mental Health: The Lions' coaching staff is also dedicated to supporting their players' mental health and well-being. They understand that football is a physically and mentally demanding game, and they actively work to create an environment where players feel comfortable discussing personal challenges or mental health concerns. The coaches make sure that players know they are not just cared for as athletes but as people. This supportive, holistic approach to coaching has been integral to creating a safe and healthy work environment where players can focus on their professional growth and personal well-being.

In the end, while each position coach and assistant coach brings their own distinct approach to leadership, undeniable threads weave them together. At the heart of their efforts lies a shared dedication to cultivating a positive, open, and dynamic culture—one that encourages growth, transparency, and mutual respect. Through their leadership, they create environments where players and staff are empowered, supported, and inspired to strive for excellence.

Chapter 5: The Players

The Detroit Lions' transformation from a struggling franchise to a rising contender in the NFC directly results from the culture cultivated by Dan Campbell, Brad Holmes, and Sheila Hamp. These leaders have played a critical role in shaping a locker room environment that values accountability, a team-first mentality, resilience, and relentless effort—principles the players have fully embraced (Payton, 2022).

At the heart of this cultural shift is Dan Campbell, whose charismatic, no-nonsense leadership has resonated deeply with the Lions' roster. Campbell's philosophy relies on mental toughness and a relentless, blue-collar work ethic. His famous "bite kneecaps" mantra is not just a catchy phrase; it reflects the attitude he instills in his players (Birkett, 2021). Campbell emphasizes a physical, competitive style of play, and his players have bought into this with unwavering commitment. Players like Amon-Ra St. Brown, whose work ethic and fiery competitiveness make him a standout, have embraced Campbell's intensity, channeling it into their play on the field. Jared Goff, often criticized for being a "game manager," has thrived under Campbell's guidance, taking on leadership and demonstrating the mental fortitude that Campbell prizes. Goff's growth is a testament to Campbell's supportive but demanding environment.

On the personnel side, Brad Holmes has built a roster that perfectly fits Campbell's culture. Holmes values character and mentality just as much as talent. Through smart draft picks and shrewd free-agent signings, Holmes has brought in players who embody the Lions' culture of resilience and accountability. Aidan Hutchinson, the Lions' first-round pick in 2022, has quickly become the face of the defense, displaying exceptional skill and the relentless motor and leadership that Holmes and Campbell covet. Hutchinson's work ethic, combined with his natural talent, represents the kind of player Holmes seeks—someone who will thrive in a system where effort and dedication are paramount.

As the team's owner, Sheila Hamp has been equally instrumental in creating a culture of stability and long-term growth. Under her leadership, the Lions have become a family-oriented organization where players contribute to the team's success. Hamp's investment in the front office, coaching staff, and player development has helped the Lions build a culture that values individual growth and collective success. This vision is reflected in how the team plays: as a cohesive unit, with every player contributing, whether David Montgomery grinding out tough yards or Frank Ragnow anchoring the offensive line with unmatched toughness (Baldoni, 2023).

In addition to the team's star players, the Lions' depth speaks to how every player on the roster has embraced this cultural shift. Craig Reynolds, often seen as a depth piece in the backfield, continues to prove his worth with a professional attitude that aligns with Campbell's focus on effort, regardless of role. Kerby Joseph has shown great promise in the secondary, fitting into a defense emphasizing teamwork and tenacity.

The coaching styles and collective culture of the Detroit Lions mesh with the individual strengths and contributions of key players, highlighting how these players fit within the team's ethos of accountability, resilience, and collaboration:

Jared Goff – Quarterback

Goff has become a more confident, efficient quarterback under Head Coach Dan Campbell. Goff's steady leadership, poise under pressure, and decision-making ability make him the perfect fit for the Lions' team-first culture. Goff's ability to adapt and manage games aligns well with the Lions' focus on mental toughness and game intelligence, creating a leadership foundation based on trust and collaboration. Goff's commitment to humility, trust, and service to others aligns perfectly with the Lions' team-first mentality. Goff's faith reminds him to serve his team, support his teammates, and lead gracefully. His reliance on faith for strength under pressure, especially when facing adversity, helps him maintain his composure and clarity on the field. This mindset fosters a culture of mutual respect, with Goff leading by example through his servant-leader approach, inspiring others to prioritize team unity over individual accolades.

Amon-Ra St. Brown – Wide Receiver

St. Brown's work ethic, attention to detail, and fierce competitiveness perfectly fit the Lions' team-first mentality. His tireless commitment to improving and his ability to perform under pressure mesh well with the Lions' growth-focused culture. His success as a top target in Detroit's offense reflects the team's culture of accountability, as St. Brown constantly holds himself to a high standard and leads by example. St. Brown is a deeply committed individual to football and his Christian values of perseverance, discipline, and love for others. His tireless work ethic and drive to improve are grounded in his belief that his talents are gifts from God, and he uses them to honor Him and help others. St. Brown's faith also encourages him to mentor others on the team, exemplifying the biblical principle of selflessness and mutual encouragement. This translates into the Lions' collaborative team environment, where his positive influence helps foster a spirit of accountability, brotherhood, and encouragement among teammates.

David Montgomery – Running Back

David Montgomery's ability to break tackles and maintain his focus on the team's goals fits seamlessly into the Lions' blue-collar ethos. He buys into the culture of hard work and selflessness, which is vital for a running back in Detroit's system, where every player contributes to the team's success. Montgomery's leadership and toughness exemplify the resilience and pride of the Lions. His belief in humility, hard work, and dedication to service extends beyond football and into all aspects of his life. His understanding that he is part of a larger purpose helps him remain focused on the collective success of the team, not individual accolades. Montgomery's faith allows him to embrace the game's challenges with perseverance and gratitude, pushing through adversity while encouraging others to do the same. His presence in the locker room reflects a spirit of servant leadership, where teammates can lean on each other for support and guidance.

Jahmyr Gibbs – Running Back

With his elite athleticism and versatility, Gibbs brings a dynamic element to Detroit's offense. His explosiveness and mental sharpness align perfectly with the Lions' commitment to versatility and adaptability. The growth-oriented culture in Detroit will help Gibbs develop his potential while maintaining a focus on team-first contributions. This attitude aligns well with the Lions' shared success and accountability ethos. Gibbs sees his athletic abilities as gifts from God, and he is committed to using them for a higher purpose, which fuels his drive for excellence. His ability to stay focused on the team's collective goals rather than personal achievement fosters an environment of shared success. By reflecting Christian values such as patience, perseverance, and humility, Gibbs serves as a role model for younger players, demonstrating how faith can enhance athletic performance and build strong relationships within the team.

Jameson Williams – Wide Receiver

Williams's rare speed and ability to stretch the field are key attributes in Detroit's offensive scheme. Despite his raw talent, Williams continues to grow within the team's discipline-focused culture, where players are encouraged to develop all facets of their game. Williams's willingness to improve and his growing chemistry with Jared Goff exemplify his embrace of the team-first mentality. Williams understands that his success on the field is part of a greater purpose, and his faith gives him the perspective needed to stay grounded. Williams focuses on positively influencing the team by uplifting his teammates and encouraging them to focus on self-improvement and collaboration. His belief in the power of prayer, trust in God's plan, and commitment to serving others enriches the Lions' culture of unity, fostering a positive, team-centered work environment.

Sam LaPorta – Tight End

LaPorta's smooth route-running and blocking abilities make him versatile in the Lions' offense. His focus on becoming a complete player mirrors the Lions' commitment to ensuring that every player contributes to the team's collective success regardless of position. LaPorta's mindset focuses on putting the needs of his team above individual success, emphasizing the importance of being a reliable, supportive teammate. His leadership reflects the biblical values of servitude and teamwork, contributing to a mutual respect and growth culture that thrives in the Lions' locker room.

Penei Sewell – Offensive Tackle

Sewell's blend of dominance, physicality, and nastiness on the field makes him an ideal fit for Hank Fraley's offensive line. Fraley's no-nonsense approach to technique, mental toughness, and offensive line cohesion perfectly complements Sewell's playing style. Sewell's development is driven by a culture emphasizing discipline, accountability, and team cohesion. As a cornerstone of the offensive line, Sewell's relentless work ethic and leadership play a significant role in building the Lions' culture of toughness and resilience. Sewell's Christian faith teaches him the values of humility, discipline, and gratitude, which are evident in his on-field play. He views his success as a means to serve his team, and he strives to be a humble leader who values collaboration and shared victory over individual glory. Sewell's belief in the power of prayer and trusting in God's timing gives him the mental fortitude to face challenges with confidence and composure. His faith-based leadership and unshakable determination help foster a team environment grounded in mutual respect, toughness, and resilience, creating an atmosphere where each player feels valued and motivated to contribute to the team's success.

Taylor Decker – Offensive Tackle

Decker brings stability and leadership to the offensive line, aligning perfectly with Hank Fraley's emphasis on strong fundamentals and communication. Decker's veteran presence and ability to set the tone on the field make him a natural fit within the Lions' culture of accountability. His focus on improving and mentoring younger players while continuing to dominate at his position embodies the team-first mentality and a commitment to excellence that defines the Lions' identity. His belief in putting others first, embracing humility, and embodying patience enables him to mentor younger players effectively. Decker's trust in God's plan gives him the peace to navigate success and failure gracefully. As a leader in the locker room, his faith-centered approach encourages a culture of love, accountability, and mutual support. His willingness to serve others and use his platform for positive change reflects the Christian principles of selflessness and community (Broder, 2023).

Graham Glasgow – Offensive Guard

Glasgow's ability to excel in both run blocking and pass protection fits well with Fraley's focus on versatility and technical precision. Glasgow is known for his leadership and adaptability, which aligns with the Lions' culture of collaborative improvement. His willingness to adjust his game and constantly work on technique makes him a key figure in maintaining the offensive line's chemistry, ensuring the offensive line operates with a strong sense of unity and accountability. He views every opportunity to improve as a chance to honor his faith and strives to be a light to those around him. His strong work ethic and commitment to teamwork are grounded in his faith, which encourages him to serve his teammates and work toward the collective good of the team. Glasgow contributes to creating a positive and supportive team culture by prioritizing unity and selflessness, reflecting the Christian principles of love and mutual encouragement.

Frank Ragnow – Center

Ragnow's leadership, physicality, and communication skills are paramount to the cohesion of the offensive line. As the anchor of the unit, Ragnow plays a crucial role in ensuring that Fraley's teachings on technique and teamwork translate into execution on the field. His focus on mental and physical toughness aligns with the Lions' discipline-first approach, and his ability to handle the responsibility of calling out protections directly reflects the Lions' culture of leadership, focus, and team cohesion. His belief in the power of humility, discipline, and service drives him to be a steady, reliable presence within the Lions' offensive line. Ragnow views his role as the center of service and strives to lead by example in his commitment to the team's goals and daily work ethic. His faith fosters a sense of unity and trust within the offensive line, helping to create a culture of collaboration where every player is focused on doing their part for the team's success (Maakaron, 2023).

Craig Reynolds – Running Back

Reynolds may not get the same spotlight as the other running backs, but his work ethic, resilience, and ability to step up make him a perfect example of the Lions' depth-focused approach. His attitude and commitment to team success are essential components of the culture of accountability the Lions are building. He understands that his role on the team is to support others and contribute in any way necessary, reflecting the Christian value of servitude. Reynolds's faith reminds him that true success is by how well he supports and elevates those around him. His quiet leadership and willingness to step up when called upon help create an environment where teammates are encouraged to put the team's needs first.

Aidan Hutchinson – Defensive End

Hutchinson's relentless pursuit, pass-rushing ability, and leadership are a perfect match for defensive line coach Terrell Williams. Hutchinson embodies the Lions' philosophy of mental toughness, physicality, and team-oriented focus. His constant desire to improve aligns with the team's focus on accountability and continuous development. Hutchinson's energy and determination make him a key player in maintaining the team's relentless effort and disciplined identity. Hutchinson's faith drives him to play with a passion for excellence, knowing that his efforts are not only for his success, but for the greater glory of God and the team's benefit. His leadership and commitment to team unity help instill a strong sense of discipline and purpose in the Lions' defense.

Brian Branch – Safety

Branch's intelligence, ball skills, and versatility in coverage and run support fit perfectly with Deshea Townsend's passing game philosophy. Branch's ability to adapt and contribute to multiple facets of the defense makes him an ideal fit for the Lions' collaborative defensive system. His approach to the game reflects the team's culture of accountability and adaptability, and where his faith encourages him to approach every play with a gratitude mindset and focus on doing his best for the team. Branch's commitment to accountability and his ability to uplift others through encouragement reflects his Christian values, helping to create a supportive and positive environment in the locker room. His faith reinforces the importance of teamwork, and his leadership in the secondary sets the tone for a defense built on collaboration and trust.

Kerby Joseph – Safety

Joseph's instincts and ability to create turnovers are essential for Detroit's defense. His development under the guidance of Townsend focuses on refining his technique and enhancing his awareness. Joseph's contributions fit seamlessly within the Lions' culture of mental toughness and leadership, where every player contributes to the defense's overall success. His growing leadership and remaining focused on the greater good encourage him to maintain perspective, even in high-pressure situations. Joseph's humility and willingness to serve others make him a natural leader within the Lions' defense, and his faith strengthens his resolve to improve continuously. His ability to create turnovers and make impactful plays reflects his commitment to his personal growth and the team's success, inspired by his Christian values of accountability and service.

Jack Campbell – Linebacker

Campbell's ability to read offenses and his physicality make him a perfect fit for linebackers coach Kelvin Sheppard's system. Sheppard's focus on developing linebackers' football IQ and instincts aligns with Campbell's approach to the game. His work ethic and adaptability perfectly match the Lions' culture of continuous improvement, where players are encouraged to learn and develop. Campbell's leadership and physicality make him a key component of Detroit's defensive future. His belief in discipline, hard work, and humility shapes his approach to football, ensuring his focus remains on the team's collective success. Campbell's faith fuels his commitment to growth and excellence, motivating him to push through challenges with perseverance and a positive attitude. His leadership in the linebacking corps is grounded in his Christian principles of servitude, encouragement, and selflessness, which foster a supportive, team-oriented environment.

Alex Anzalone – Linebacker

Anzalone's leadership, versatility, and ability to excel in both run defense and pass coverage make him a key figure in the Lions' defense. Under Sheppard's guidance, Anzalone continues to develop his leadership skills, which are vital to maintaining team cohesion. Anzalone embodies the Lions' culture of hard work, mental toughness, and selflessness, often serving as a mentor for younger players. Anzalone's commitment to his teammates and dedication to continuous improvement reflect his Christian values of service and humility. His leadership helps cultivate a team culture based on mutual support, discipline, and trust.

The Lions' players have bought into the vision set by Campbell, Holmes, and Hamp. They have embraced a team-first mentality, understanding that individual success is secondary to collective achievement. Under the guidance of these three leaders, the Lions have established a foundation of trust, mental toughness, and selflessness that is driving them toward success. The team's resurgence is not just about talent—it is about the culture that Campbell, Holmes, and Hamp have worked tirelessly to create, and it is clear that the players are fully invested in making it a lasting success.

Chapter 6: Rising from the Rust

Detroit, the Motor City, is more than just a place—it is a living, breathing testament to resilience, work ethic, and community spirit. Its people, fans, and culture embody a raw, unapologetic grit defined by a commitment to hard work, a relentless pursuit of excellence, and a deep pride in doing things the right way. Whether on the football field, in the factories, or in the neighborhoods, Detroiters approach life with an unflinching determination, striving to overcome obstacles, rebuild, and push forward—always with humility and integrity. In many ways, the spirit of Detroit mirrors workplaces with positive cultures—where the emphasis is on collaboration, mutual respect, and a shared commitment to doing things well, no matter the challenge.

Detroit has long been synonymous with industry, innovation, and hard work. For over a century, the city has been home to some of the most iconic businesses in America, with Ford, General Motors, Chrysler, Detroit Diesel Corporation, Carhartt, and American Axle representing the heart of Detroit's manufacturing heritage. These companies are pillars of the Detroit economy and reflect the city's identity—defined by humility, a relentless work ethic, and a deep commitment to doing things the right way.

The legacy of these businesses runs parallel to the history of the city itself—one of resilience, reinvention, and dedication to quality and craftsmanship. In Detroit, these businesses are more than just corporations—they are institutions woven into the very fabric of the city. From the assembly lines of the auto industry to the rugged, durable clothing worn by hardworking people, these businesses have exemplified the values that define the Motor City: a commitment to excellence, an unwavering work ethic, and humility born from the city's blue-collar roots.

At the core of Detroit's identity is an unyielding grit—a resilience forged through decades of economic shifts, industrial decline, and the perseverance required to rebuild. The city has faced challenges and setbacks, yet it continues to push forward, refusing to be defined by its past struggles. This tenacity is seen in every corner of the city—from the workers in the factories to the students in the classrooms, from the entrepreneurs in the tech startups to the community leaders fighting for change. This same resilience is evident in individuals who live out Christlike principles—believing in redemption, second chances, and the power of faith to overcome adversity. Like a thriving workplace culture, setbacks serve as opportunities for growth; Detroiters understand that success does not come quickly. It requires long hours, persistence, and, often, working through adversity.

The city's labor history, symbolized by the auto industry's rise and the union movements that powered it, reflects the values Detroit holds dear: hard work, sacrifice, and a belief that a job well done is worth its weight in pride. These principles are at the heart of Detroit's blue-collar mentality and the core of effective, Christ-centered leadership in any environment. In the workplace and the community, there is an understanding that success is not a given—it is earned through sweat, sacrifice, and a commitment to serving others. Whether it is a business owner taking pride in the products they make or a sports fan celebrating a hard-fought victory, the humility that defines Detroit is reflected in the quiet confidence of its people.

Ford Motor Company is a legendary brand deeply intertwined with Detroit's history and spirit. Founded in 1903 by Henry Ford, the company revolutionized the automobile industry by introducing the moving assembly line (Womack et al., 2007). This feat transformed how cars were produced and changed the course of history for workers and the American middle class. Ford's legacy is not just about creating the Model T; it is about creating jobs, building communities, and investing in the people who make the company what it is.

Ford's commitment to Detroit and its workers runs deep. The company has consistently invested in the city, even during economic uncertainty, as part of a broader vision to make great cars and positively impact the community. An example was in 2002 when the Detroit Lions moved their home from the Pontiac Silverdome to Ford Field in downtown Detroit (Cavaiani, 2015). Ford's founder, Henry Ford, was known for paying his workers a fair wage and setting standards for labor rights that were groundbreaking at the time. His philosophy that workers should be able to afford the products they make is a core value that continues to shape Ford's corporate culture today (Lewis, 1976).

Ford's continued presence in Detroit reminds us of the company's commitment to doing things the right way. The company focuses on sustainability, innovation, and community while never losing sight of its humble beginnings in the Motor City. Ford remains committed to its workers, many of whom are the sons and daughters of the original factory laborers, carrying forward the legacy of hard work, determination, and pride in building innovative and durable products.

General Motors (GM), founded in 1908, is arguably one of the most recognized names in Detroit and American manufacturing. It has long symbolized the city's industrial prowess and innovation. While GM has undergone significant changes over the decades—weathering economic downturns, shifting consumer demands, and technological revolutions—the company has remained true to its blue-collar and hardworking character. These traits are front and center in some of their most notable core values: "One Team: Working together despite the distance. Be Bold: Respectfully speaking up, exchanging feedback, and boldly sharing ideas without fear. It's on Me: Taking personal responsibility for your work and contributions to our culture. Winning with Integrity: Doing the right thing, even when it is difficult" (General Motors, n.d.).

GM's long-standing relationship with the city is rooted in its commitment to creating good jobs, empowering workers, and building products that stand the test of time. The automaker has been a cornerstone of Detroit's economy for decades, employing generations of families and shaping the city's identity. Through it all, GM's leadership has emphasized the importance of integrity, quality, and innovation—doing things the right way, even when it is not the easiest or most profitable option.

General Motors' workforce is a testament to the blue-collar ethic that defines Detroit. The company has long been committed to providing fair wages, job security, and opportunities for workers to advance, regardless of their background. This focus on respect, hard work, and fair practices has earned GM the loyalty of its employees and the community's trust.

Chrysler, now part of Stellantis, is another keystone in the automotive industry that carries the spirit of Detroit forward. Since 1925, Chrysler has been creating vehicles that combine performance, style, and practicality (Beresford, 2021). Known for its grit, Chrysler has faced financial difficulties, but like Detroit, it has always found a way to reinvent itself. The company's resilience mirrors the city's ability to rebound from economic setbacks, and its people are integral to that success. Chrysler's factories are often considered a model for manufacturing efficiency and quality, with a workforce that brings unmatched passion and dedication to every vehicle built. The company's commitment to its employees is evident by an unmatched workplace culture that emphasizes collaboration, respect, and a focus on empowering the people who keep the wheels of the city turning.

In addition to focusing on productivity, Chrysler has become increasingly forward-thinking, integrating new technologies, sustainability efforts, and employee wellness programs that speak to its ongoing investment in the community. Whether the workers on the assembly line or the engineers designing the next generation of vehicles, Chrysler continues to prove that its greatest asset is the people who make up the company—people who share the same grit and determination that define Detroit itself.

Detroit Diesel Corporation is another pillar of Detroit's manufacturing might. Since its founding in 1938, Detroit Diesel has built a reputation for producing some of the most durable and high-performance diesel engines. Its engines power the vehicles that deliver goods across the country, from long-haul trucks to buses that carry workers in and out of the city daily. Like its parent company, Daimler Trucks North America, Detroit Diesel has evolved, but its focus on quality, precision, and innovation has never wavered.

What truly sets Detroit Diesel apart is its deep connection to the city's blue-collar workforce. The company's commitment to creating a workplace culture emphasizing safety, respect, and continuous improvement is unparalleled. Workers at Detroit Diesel do not just build engines—they build the future of transportation and infrastructure. The company's culture is one of loyalty and mutual respect, where employees are seen as part of the production process and as vital contributors to the company's ongoing success. Detroit Diesel's workforce is built on pride—pride in their work, pride in the city, and pride in continuing the tradition of excellence that has defined Detroit's manufacturing sector for generations.

Carhartt, founded in 1889, is a brand that embodies Detroit's values like few others. Known for its tough, rugged workwear, Carhartt has long been the go-to choice for those whose livelihoods depend on their ability to work hard and get the job done. The company has remained family-owned for over a century, maintaining its commitment to quality craftsmanship and durability, values that are deeply rooted in Detroit's work ethic.

Carhartt's humble beginnings in Detroit were born from a desire to create durable clothing that could withstand the most challenging jobs. The company has stayed true to that original vision, crafting high-quality workwear for generations of workers. Whether it is a line worker in an auto plant, a construction worker on a Detroit skyline, or an artist building the city's new cultural centers, Carhartt's clothing is for those who understand what it means to work hard, day in and day out.

Carhartt's continued success reflects its humble, no-frills approach to business. The company is deeply embedded in Detroit's culture, making its mark globally without compromising its commitment to hard work and quality. Carhartt is a perfect example of Detroit's gritty, humble spirit—building something that lasts, doing it the right way, and honoring the genuine values of the city.

American Axle & Manufacturing (AAM) is another key player in Detroit's manufacturing legacy. Founded in 1994, AAM produces automotive driveline and drivetrain systems, including axles, driveshafts, and chassis components. Though a younger company than GM, Ford, and Carhartt, AAM has quickly become a cornerstone of Detroit's industrial landscape. With manufacturing facilities in the Detroit metro area, AAM's work has kept the city's automotive industry humming.

American Axle embodies the values of Detroit's workforce: hardworking, innovative, and committed to excellence. The company operates with the same blue-collar mentality synonymous with the city for generations. AAM's commitment to Detroit is evident in its partnerships with local workers and investment in the city's growth. It is another example of a company that understands the value of the people who make its products and the importance of providing jobs that support families and communities.

The company's focus on creating high-quality components that power the vehicles driven by millions of people worldwide reflects the grit and determination that define Detroit. AAM's focus on innovation and excellence and its commitment to the community make it vital to the city's industrial heartbeat.

These companies—Ford, GM, Chrysler, Detroit Diesel, Carhartt, and American Axle—are not just businesses; they are vital pieces of Detroit's identity. These companies demonstrate that a strong foundation built on hard work, perseverance, and a dedication to excellence can pave the way to success. Much like the Detroit Lions, who have worked to establish a sustainable and winning culture for years, these businesses embody the spirit of resilience that defines Detroit. Over time, the Lions have invested in creating a culture centered on development, accountability, and pride in representing the city. Whether it is through focusing on strong leadership, supporting their players, or building long-term success, they mirror the hardworking ethos that permeates the businesses of Detroit.

What sets these businesses apart is not just their products—it is their people. The workers who spend long hours on assembly lines, the designers who innovate and push boundaries, and the leaders who drive their companies forward all share a commitment to excellence and to Detroit. Nevertheless, beyond their drive for success, these individuals also embody values that transcend the workplace. Much like Christ's example of servant leadership, these men and women operate with humility, putting the needs of others before their own and dedicating themselves to work that serves the community and creates a lasting impact. Their approach to work is rooted in integrity, honesty, and a deep sense of responsibility to those around them.

This humility is reflected in how fans back their teams, particularly the Detroit Lions. While Detroiters are passionate, they remain realistic—acknowledging their team's struggles but still showing steadfast loyalty. They cheer for victories and the effort and the heart their players put into every game. This mirrors the dynamic of workplace teams and organizations where success is not simply about individual accolades, but about how each member contributes to the collective effort with dedication and heart. Detroit's sports fans are some of the most loyal in the country, sticking with their teams through thick and thin and showing up year after year, season after season, without the expectation of instant success—but with the belief that the right work ethic will eventually pay off. In this way, the Lions and their fans are a microcosm of the broader Detroit ethos—unpretentious, unrelenting, and ready to rise again, no matter the obstacles. Like an individual who lives out Christlike perseverance, these fans embody the strength to endure through trials with faith and hope that victory will come.

In Detroit, there is a deep understanding that to succeed, one must choose to outwork everyone else. It is the belief that no task is too small, no challenge too big, and that even when the odds appear too much to overcome, hard work and perseverance will always provide a fighting chance. This spirit of perseverance and faith in the process is also central to workplaces prioritizing long-term goals over quick wins. The city's comeback story includes individuals and families who have again poured sweat, blood, and tears into making Detroit a place of pride. Whether it is the tradespeople who helped rebuild the city's infrastructure, the artists who turned empty buildings into vibrant galleries, or the community organizers who fought to restore neighborhoods, Detroiters have shown time and time again that they will roll up their sleeves and get the job done. This work ethic is not limited to the factory floors or construction sites—it is visible in every aspect of life. It is present in the teachers working long hours to ensure the next generation succeeds, the small business owners who pour their hearts into their shops, and the coaches and players who understand there is more to the recipe of success than talent alone, much like the believers who embrace Christ's example of selflessness, those who embody a positive workplace culture understand that true success comes from a collective effort to persist, no matter the difficulties faced along the way.

From the passionate cheers at Ford Field to the pride displayed by Lions fans in every corner of the city, Detroiters understand that their success aligns with the success of their neighbors, communities, and teams. There is no room for divisiveness in Detroit—there is only a shared commitment to doing things right, working hard, and pushing forward together. There is an undeniable sense of unity. People come together, work together, and encourage each other, knowing that the community's collective strength is what makes the city great. This sense of togetherness is reflected in the Lions' fan base, where the diverse mix of backgrounds and stories all come together to support the exact cause: the pride of Detroit. The kind of unity that fosters this collective strength is similar to the bonds seen in workplaces that prioritize collaboration and mutual respect. Every member of the team is valued and supported in their role. Like a Christ-centered community, this unity is about more than just showing up; it is about genuinely lifting each other up, even in difficult times. This makes Detroit more than just a city; it is a living, breathing example of how people can come together, support one another, and rise above challenges in the same way we see Christlike values guiding communities and organizations toward success.

Chapter 7: The Reality

Fortune 500 companies prioritizing and seriously developing a positive, inclusive, and professional work culture generally see significantly higher employee satisfaction, engagement, and retention rates (Kotter & Heskett, 2011). Research has consistently shown that companies with strong cultures outperform their peers in several key areas:

Higher Employee Engagement: Companies with a well-defined, positive culture tend to have more engaged employees. For example, organizations like Google, Salesforce, and HubSpot invest heavily in fostering open communication, work-life balance, and growth opportunities. Engaged employees are more motivated and productive, contributing to overall business success.

Lower Turnover: Companies that prioritize culture usually experience lower turnover rates (Deal & Kennedy, 2008). Microsoft, for example, emphasizes growth opportunities, inclusivity, and employee well-being, leading to high retention rates. Employees who feel respected, supported, and valued are less likely to leave.

Increased Innovation: A culture that values creativity, feedback, and collaboration tends to foster innovation. Companies like Apple, Smartsheet, and 3M encourage employees to think outside the box and provide an environment where new ideas can flourish. This results in enhanced product development and improved market differentiation.

More Substantial Brand Reputation: A positive internal culture often translates into an enhanced external brand reputation. Employees at companies with strong cultures are likely to share their positive experiences, boosting the company's employer brand and attracting top talent. Patagonia and Ben & Jerry's are examples of companies whose strong ethical values and company culture align with their external messaging.

Improved Financial Performance: Studies have shown a direct link between employee satisfaction with company culture and improved financial outcomes (Chang et al., 2021). American Express and Adobe have shown that companies that focus on creating a supportive, engaging work environment experience higher productivity, profitability, and growth.

Adaptability and Resilience: A strong organizational culture helps companies weather challenges (Sørensen). During times of crisis or change, companies like Zoom Video Communications and Netflix have maintained employee satisfaction by ensuring clear communication, flexibility, and continued investment in employee well-being, leading to resilience and quick recovery.

The performance of these companies shows that when culture is a key focus, employee satisfaction is significantly improved, which drives organizational success across multiple dimensions. Ultimately, a culture that aligns with employees' values and needs creates a happier workforce and contributes to sustained business growth. Organizations that embrace Christlike values, such as compassion and teamwork, tend to cultivate environments where people are supported, morale is high, and retention rates improve. Simple yet powerful examples of these principles include listening attentively to employees' needs, offering support during difficult times, and fostering an inclusive and collaborative atmosphere. When companies and teams act with integrity and a servant-leadership mindset, they create a culture that drives success and nurtures the well-being of all involved.

Chapter 8: Into the Light or Darkness?

Faith, especially in Jesus Christ, is a guiding light that shapes a healthy, purpose-driven workplace culture. Just as light illuminates the path and enables clear vision, faith in Christ brings clarity, purpose, and direction to our work and relationships. It fosters an environment of trust, compassion, and collaboration, allowing individuals to thrive and work together in harmony. In contrast, the absence of faith is akin to darkness, where confusion, fear, and negativity can take root. Darkness, representing the influence of Satan, seeks to obscure truth, disrupt unity, and sow discord among individuals. Without the light of Christ, the void allows hostile forces to influence one's thoughts, actions, and interactions, undermining a positive and purposeful workplace. By examining the contrast between light (faith in Jesus) and darkness (Satan's influence), we gain deeper insight into how faith's presence or absence can significantly shape a workplace's dynamics and the quality of its relationships. Where faith flourishes, so does peace and productivity; where darkness prevails, so does conflict and division.

Purpose Beyond Profit: A Higher Calling

Without faith, people may become entirely driven by self-interest, profit, and personal gain, which can easily lead to unethical behavior, manipulation, and a cutthroat work environment. This self-centered focus mirrors the influence of dark forces, which encourage selfishness, greed, and the prioritization of individual desires over collective well-being. When driven by these forces, employees and leaders may disregard the higher calling of serving others or contributing to a greater purpose. Millennials and Gen Z increasingly seek purpose and fulfillment in their careers (Chala et al., 2022). A lack of faith-based purpose in the workplace can create a culture that fails to engage them, leaving them disconnected and disillusioned. Older generations, who may still find value in long-term career advancement and stability, may also struggle with lacking a sense of community or mission.

Servant Leadership: Empowering Others, Not Just Leading

Leadership can become authoritarian, driven by ego, power, and a desire to control without faith. This reflects Satan's destructive qualities, who seeks to dominate and destroy rather than uplift. A lack of servant leadership creates an environment where employees feel disposable, unimportant, or coerced into compromising their values. Workers valuing empathy and transparency may struggle with leaders focusing on personal power or authority. Older generations may find such a leadership style familiar, but may also experience burnout if it results in an overly demanding and unsupportive work environment.

Ethical Foundation and Integrity

If individuals fail to seek a meaningful relationship with God, they may become susceptible to temptation and corruption. A lack of integrity leads to dishonesty, fraud, and unethical behavior that ultimately erodes trust and harms relationships. Dark forces thrive in environments where lies, manipulation, and deception are tolerated or ignored. Younger employees, particularly those attuned to social justice and ethical practices, may feel disillusioned in environments where dishonesty persists. Older employees, while possibly more accustomed to business practices of previous eras, may still recognize the erosion of trust as a threat to a stable and functional work environment.

Community and Unity: Building a Family-Like Environment

Without faith, workplaces may become fragmented, with employees isolated or competing rather than collaborating. A lack of faith creates an environment where division, envy, and distrust can thrive, undermining team spirit and community. This mirrors the divisiveness and destruction wrought by dark forces, which seek to break relationships and foster discord. Generations that value collaboration and inclusivity can avoid organizations that lack a strong, faith-driven community. Older generations, while perhaps more familiar with hierarchical structures, can still suffer from a lack of unity, feeling disconnected or unsupported.

Resilience in the Face of Adversity

Adversity can lead to despair, burnout, and a sense of hopelessness in the absence of faith. Without the grounding of faith, employees may feel overwhelmed by setbacks and unable to cope, a state that aligns with the forces of darkness, which aim to lead individuals into despair and defeat (Wollard, 2011). Younger generations, who may face economic and personal challenges in an unstable world, may lack the resilience that faith provides, leading to higher turnover or disengagement. Older generations might struggle to adapt to rapid changes in the workplace, further weakened by the absence of faith and hope.

Forgiveness and Conflict Resolution

Bitterness and resentment can grow without faith, leading to a toxic work environment where conflicts escalate and relationships deteriorate. The inability to forgive is akin to the work of dark forces that seek to perpetuate anger, division, and hatred, rather than peace and reconciliation. Younger workers may struggle in environments where conflicts are left unresolved or where forgiveness is not encouraged. Older generations might have a more challenging time navigating the modern workplace's emphasis on emotional intelligence and conflict resolution, especially without the framework of faith guiding them.

Well-Being and Compassion

A lack of faith can lead to disregarding employees' well-being, focusing instead on productivity and profit. This mirrors dark forces that exploit individuals for their gain, stripping them of dignity, health, and peace. With a growing focus on mental health and well-being, younger generations are susceptible to environments that neglect personal care. Older generations may struggle to express their needs or see the importance of compassionate care, potentially leading to physical and emotional burnout.

The absence of faith, particularly religious faith, creates an environment that can quickly become a breeding ground for the destructive forces of darkness. Without the grounding influence of faith, individuals and organizations are more likely to fall prey to selfishness, conflict, and despair. In contrast, when workplaces embrace faith-based principles—especially those rooted in the teachings of Jesus Christ—they foster a culture of service, compassion, integrity, and unity. The result is a workplace where employees thrive professionally and are supported spiritually and emotionally, creating a healthier, more purposeful environment for all generations. The question becomes, what are we influencing ourselves with daily that shapes our individual selves more toward the light or the darkness?

The concept that celebrities, professional athletes, government officials, and highly followed social media accounts wield tremendous influence over public thought, culture, and values has always been prevalent (Marshall, 2014). Whether or not intentionally, they set moral and cultural examples for millions. Through their actions, choices, and ideals, they either align with Jesus Christ—the embodiment of truth, love, and service—or with the Dark One, who leads people down paths of deceit, greed, self-obsession, and destruction. Celebrities are role models for the masses, impacting how we view success, morality, and relationships. There is a stark contrast between the teachings of Jesus, who emphasizes selflessness, love, humility, and truth, and the destructive nature of the Dark One, who fuels pride, ego, and selfish ambition.

Let's explore a couple of well-branded individuals, examining their values, actions, and public personas to determine whether they are aligned with Jesus Christ's teachings or with the Dark One's destructive influence. We can frame the ideals and influences of celebrities, evaluating their actions and messages through a spiritual lens of light (Christ) versus darkness (the devil) and celebrities' role in shaping culture.

Russell Brand: A charismatic comedian and actor known for his rebellious nature, Brand has undergone a significant transformation. Once notorious for his hedonistic lifestyle and outlandish behavior, Brand has embraced spirituality and frequently shares his thoughts on self-awareness, mindfulness, and social change. He openly critiques materialism, consumerism, and the injustices of modern society, often using his platform to challenge people to think critically. While Brand's spiritual journey and critiques of societal structures seem to align with the search for truth and inner peace, his past indulgence in pride and self-glorification points to the constant tension between worldly temptation and spiritual awakening. His current path reflects Christlike ideals in some respects, but his earlier fame-driven antics remind one how easily the darkness of pride and excess can seduce one. It's been remarkable to see how someone can be lifted into the light from darkness (Mastro, 2024).

Chris Pratt: Known for his transition from comedic roles in *Parks and Recreation* to blockbuster hits like *Guardians of the Galaxy* and *Jurassic World*, Chris Pratt has undergone a public transformation. He has openly discussed his Christian faith and personal spiritual growth journey, attributing much of his success and strength to his relationship with God. Pratt uses his platform to promote gratitude, humility, and positivity, often sharing his beliefs on family, personal responsibility, and the importance of prayer. His commitment to faith and vulnerability in addressing struggles like body image and mental health resonates with Christ's teachings on self-reflection, grace, and humility.

However, Pratt has faced criticism for his involvement in controversies related to his church and some of his outspoken views, which sometimes conflict with messages of inclusivity and compassion. While his faith and values generally align with Christ's message of love, there remains a tension between fame's temptation to focus on self-promotion and the call to walk humbly and serve others (Darby, 2023).

These individuals have faced unique struggles and triumphs in their public lives. In evaluating their public personas through a spiritual lens, we see they have moments of aligning with Christ's values—whether through personal growth, philanthropy, or advocacy for justice. Yet, there are also temptations and challenges tied to their fame that pull them toward vanity, self-glorification, and materialism. These examples highlight the complexity of fame and the ongoing tension between light and darkness, showcasing how even the most influential figures must constantly navigate the pull of worldly distractions and the call to selflessness and service.

Celebrities wield immense power to shape culture, either as instruments of good or conduits of evil. Their influence is profound, as they can guide millions of followers through their words, actions, and choices. This serves as a reminder for readers to weigh the values promoted by celebrities against the teachings of Jesus Christ. Just as all individuals must choose between the light of Christ and the darkness of Satan, celebrities, too, must decide whether to live for the Kingdom of God or the Kingdom of the Devil. Their choices resonate beyond their lives, impacting the hearts and minds of those who look up to them as role models.

In the light of Christ, celebrities can lead others toward righteousness, offering a beacon of hope, truth, and love. Through their actions and choices, they can inspire their followers to seek the Kingdom of God and reflect His glory in the world. However, in the darkness of Satan's influence, the choices they make can steer people away from the light, leading them into confusion, sin, and despair. The values they promote, whether aligned with the teachings of Christ or the enticements of the devil, will ultimately contribute to either the building of God's kingdom or the destruction of souls.

As consumers of celebrity culture, we must be mindful of these individuals' power and be discerning in the examples we allow to shape our lives. We must recognize celebrities' influence in guiding moral standards and understand that their choices, whether good or evil, ripple through society. This structure encourages readers to reflect on the moral decisions of celebrities—both past and present—and consider how those choices align with Christian teachings and the ultimate truth of the Gospel. In doing so, it is crucial to thoughtfully examine the values we embrace and how they reflect the light of Christ versus the darkness of Satan's pull.

Chapter 9: I♥U➡

The path forward requires us to break down the concept of toxic workplace culture and how the works of the devil align. In addition, understanding human history more deeply than ever is so we can grasp how different generational labels and communication styles are different, as each generation has unique values, concerns, and communication preferences.

1. Baby Boomers (Born 1946–1964)

Communication Style: Baby Boomers appreciate clarity, directness, and a sense of authority. They grew up in an era where respect for hierarchy and work ethic were paramount (Zemke et al., 2013). Many Baby Boomers have long careers, making them experienced in recognizing both healthy and toxic workplace behaviors. They often value loyalty, tradition, and teamwork.

Message to Boomers: "Throughout their career, Boomers have seen firsthand how toxic workplaces can take a toll—where misleading promises, division, and greed create environments that undermine teamwork, integrity, and employee morale. For Boomers, nothing is more damaging than working under a leader who abuses their power or creates an atmosphere of fear. Situations of conflict, unresolved issues, and overwork have led to burnout. It is like a cancer that eats away at productivity and unity. Furthermore, the worst part is that these situations often mirror the deceptive works of evil—where exploitation and manipulation thrive. When leadership is motivated by self-interest or greed, the team's success becomes secondary, just like the devil's goal is to steal, kill, and destroy relationships. Today, we can do better by creating workplaces that embody honesty, collaboration, and compassion. Let us stand for integrity and respect at work so the next generation of employees does not have to experience what we did."

2. Generation X (Born 1965–1980)

Communication Style: Generation X values independence, pragmatism, and authenticity. They experienced the rise of technology, and many are now in leadership positions. They tend to value work-life balance, directness, and results, and they may have a realist outlook on corporate culture due to their exposure to both the positive and negative sides of working life (Zemke et al., 2013).

Message to Gen X: "As someone who has experienced the grind of corporate life and the rise of tech and innovation, Gen X has seen the negative effects of toxic work cultures—where companies prioritize profits over people. Deception, greed, and unaccountable leadership exemplify how workplace toxicity can creep in, leading to disempowerment, burnout, and exploitation. Many workplaces still perpetuate these harmful dynamics, which ultimately sow division and create mistrust among teams. Like the devil's work that feeds on lies and despair, toxic environments erode the trust necessary for success. Experiences and real-world perspectives show us that integrity and accountability can turn the tide. Let us build workplaces focusing on empowerment and real collaboration, where transparency and ethical leadership are the foundations of success."

3. Millennials (Born 1981–1996)

Communication Style: Millennials have a values-driven approach to work. They are motivated by purpose, social justice, and mental health awareness. They are tech-savvy and expect openness, flexibility, and respect for their individuality. They are also more vocal about calling out toxic workplaces (Zemke et al., 2013).

Message to Millennials: "You have seen it firsthand—workplaces that preach work-life balance but exploit your time and energy. Millennials worked under leaders who made false promises, fostered unhealthy competition, or used power to manipulate and control. These toxic cultures not only stifle creativity and productivity but also take a toll on mental health. Like the devil's work, which thrives on division, greed, and deception, toxic leadership and a lack of integrity can leave one feeling isolated and hopeless. The good news is that social tools can call out these unethical practices through Glassdoor reviews, LinkedIn posts, or even direct conversations. Millennials want to work for transparent, compassionate, and mission-driven companies—where values like authenticity, well-being, and community matter. It is time to turn the tables and build organizations where empowerment and respect are key, and leadership prioritizes people over profits."

4. Generation Z (Born 1997–2012)

Communication Style: Generation Z is digital-native, socially conscious, and incredibly vocal about its values. It seeks meaningful work, inclusivity, and mental health support. Generation Z often expresses itself through social media platforms and demands transparency and accountability from employers. It is direct, engaged, and not afraid to call out injustices (Henry & Shannon, 2023).

Message to Gen Z: "You have grown up in a world where social justice and mental health are at the forefront of every conversation. Gen Z knows that a toxic workplace is not just about long hours or unfair wages—it is about manipulation, misinformation, and the abuse of power. The devil's work, as described in spiritual texts, thrives on deception and division, and we see this play out in corporate settings where exploitation and unhealthy competition tear people down. Gen Z does not stand for these practices and should not have to. Companies that foster inauthenticity, discrimination, or abuse of power tend to breed burnout and resentment. Gen Z looks for a culture of inclusivity, transparency, and well-being—where people can bring their authentic selves to work and feel supported. Gen Z is part of a movement that demands companies embrace ethical practices and prioritize their employees' well-being above all else."

Across all generations, false promises and unrealistic expectations at work resonate strongly. People want workplaces to mirror their values. Baby Boomers and Gen X may frame this as a matter of integrity and trust, while Millennials and Gen Z see it as a need for transparency and honesty in leadership. Gen X and Boomers recognize the destructive nature of unhealthy competition and disunity in the workplace, while Millennials and Gen Z are more vocal about collaboration, community, and teamwork. These are universal issues that cross generational lines. However, it is more likely to be challenged openly today through social media, especially by Millennials and Gen Z. Baby Boomers and Gen X may have encountered these issues but might not have had the platforms to expose them as openly.

The evil works of the devil, as described in religious texts, often align with negative behaviors in modern workplaces—deception, division, abuse of power, greed, and hopelessness. These toxic dynamics are now being exposed more widely on social media. By framing these issues within generational contexts, we can see how each group interprets, challenges, and reacts to these toxic behaviors uniquely. Ultimately, the push for better work cultures across all generations is clear: workplaces should reflect honesty, collaboration, respect, and empowerment, focusing on fostering well-being, transparency, and ethical leadership.

Chapter 10: The Power of Free Will

Free will refers to the ability of individuals to make choices that are not predetermined or influenced solely by external forces or fate. It is the capacity to act independently, make decisions, and take actions based on desires, intentions, and reasoning. From a psychological standpoint, free will is often discussed in terms of decision-making processes and self-control. With its complex network of neurons and cognitive functions, the human brain plays a significant role in making choices. While we may feel like we have free will, our brain's functions are influenced by unconscious processes, emotions, and biases that may limit our genuine autonomy.

Research in psychology and neuroscience suggests that unconscious factors or biases may influence many of our decisions. For example, the brain may decide before we are consciously aware of it, raising the question whether we truly have control over our actions or if they are merely reactions to stimuli. Some neuroscientists argue that genetic and neurological factors heavily influence our actions. For instance, our genetic makeup, brain chemistry, and past experiences might dictate our decisions, challenging the idea that we have complete control over our choices (Roskies, 2006).

From a theological perspective, many religions also engage with the concept of free will, often tying it to moral responsibility and divine judgment. In Christianity, for example, free will is seen as a gift from God, allowing humans to choose between good and evil. This freedom is necessary for moral responsibility, as individuals are held accountable for their choices.

In Islam, free will is seen as a gift, with humans having the ability to choose their actions. However, Allah is considered the ultimate authority, and some interpretations suggest that divine providence still influences human will. Other religions, such as Hinduism and Buddhism, frame free will in terms of karma and the choices individuals make that affect their future lives, with varying levels of freedom depending on one's spiritual understanding.

Free will is foundational to concepts like personal responsibility, justice, and accountability in legal and societal contexts. Laws typically assume that individuals can make choices and should be held accountable for their actions, such as in criminal justice systems, where people are judged based on their decisions (Jones, 2003).

The debate about whether free will exists is ongoing and often philosophical. Some argue that free will is essential to understanding morality, responsibility, and self-determination. Others point to the deterministic forces of biology, society, and environment that shape our choices. Free will is a complex and multifaceted concept that raises significant questions about responsibility, morality, and human nature. Whether we are free to choose or whether external factors influence our choices is a topic of ongoing debate. While some believe in absolute freedom of choice, others argue that our actions result from predetermined factors, such as genetics, environment, or subconscious influences. Ultimately, the concept of free will invites us to reflect on our understanding of human autonomy and accountability in a world where various forces—biological, theological, societal, and philosophical—come into play.

As we explore the role of free will in shaping our choices and actions, it becomes clear that the environments we inhabit—personal or professional—can heavily influence how we exercise that freedom. In particular, the choices we make within the workplace can foster an atmosphere of support and growth or perpetuate toxicity and harm. Just as internal desires and external pressures shape individual actions, the cultures created within organizations are shaped by leadership, values, and the collective behavior of employees. These organizational dynamics can either uplift or undermine the well-being of workers. When this hostile environment prevails, it often leads to outcomes that mirror destructive forces identified in various moral and religious teachings. The concept of the devil's evil works in Christian theology is often tied to values and behaviors that oppose good, integrity, and the well-being of individuals and communities. When we apply these teachings to the context of modern workplace culture, particularly in an age where social media platforms allow employees to share their experiences openly, we can draw disturbing parallels between the destructive forces of negativity, division, and exploitation that we sometimes see in toxic work environments and what religious traditions identify as the "works of the devil."

To explore this connection, let us first consider the nature of evil works described in Christian theology and how they relate to harmful behaviors and toxic cultures in the workplace.

1. Deception and Misinformation

The devil is often described as a deceiver who twists the truth to confuse, manipulate, and lead people astray. In John 8:44, Jesus describes the devil as "the father of lies," highlighting the destructive power of deceit in undermining relationships and trust. In many toxic work environments, employees may face misleading communication, false promises, or unrealistic expectations from leadership. For example, companies may overpromise growth opportunities, a work-life balance, or job security during recruitment, only for new hires to experience a different reality once they start. Employees may also find their contributions misrepresented or exploited by their superiors. In the modern age of social media, disgruntled employees increasingly expose these misalignments on social media platforms, sharing their stories of being misled, lied to, or manipulated by employers. These deceptive practices create distrust and a sense of betrayal, destroying morale and creating a toxic work environment.

2. Division and Discord

A key characteristic of the devil's influence is to sow division among people, turning them against one another and creating discord in communities. In Matthew 12:25, Jesus warns, "Every kingdom divided against itself will be ruined, and every city or household divided against itself will not stand." The devil thrives in environments where people turn against each other. In toxic workplaces, division and infighting are rampant. Leaders may play employees against one another, pit teams against each other, or encourage competition at the cost of collaboration. This creates an atmosphere where people are focused on self-preservation or getting ahead at the expense of others. Favoritism, discrimination, and gossip often flourish in these environments, leading to a fractured workplace with low morale, high turnover, and a lack of team cohesion.

3. Exploitation and Abuse of Power

Another destructive force associated with the devil is the abuse of power. Satan seeks to dominate and control others through manipulation, coercion, and exploitation. In 1 Peter 5:8, the devil is depicted as a "roaring lion looking for someone to devour," emphasizing the destructive power of unchecked authority and dominance over others. In workplaces where exploitation and abuse of power are present, employees often feel oppressed, undervalued, and exhausted. Unrealistic demands, overwork, and a lack of appreciation mark these environments. Power dynamics are skewed, with leadership often exercising authority through fear or intimidation rather than empowerment and respect. Toxic bosses may take credit for the work of others, micromanage, or gaslight employees to keep them in constant confusion and self-doubt. This exploitation of power can lead to burnout, mental health struggles, and lack of job satisfaction, as employees feel trapped in a system where their needs and well-being are secondary to the company's bottom line.

4. Envy, Jealousy, and Competition

Satan also instills envy and jealousy, as these emotions breed hatred and destruction. James 3:16 says, "For where you have envy and selfish ambition, there you find disorder and every evil practice." Jealousy makes people focus on others' failures instead of their growth, causing division and toxicity. In toxic workplaces, employees are often encouraged to compete against each other instead of working together toward common goals. This envy-driven competition can create an atmosphere of backstabbing, undermining, and cutthroat behavior. Rather than celebrating collective wins, these organizations foster a mindset of self-interest and individual achievement at all costs. This environment encourages employees to withhold information, sabotage others' work, or seek to climb the corporate ladder through manipulative tactics rather than merit. The result is a lack of trust, morale, and unity.

5. Discouragement and Hopelessness

One of the devil's goals is to create a sense of hopelessness and despair in people, making them feel like their efforts are in vain. In John 10:10, Jesus contrasts the devil's work with his mission: "The thief comes only to steal and kill and destroy; I have come that they may have life, and have it to the full." The devil's influence leads to despair, while Christ offers hope and abundance. A culture of negativity and hopelessness permeates workplaces where leadership fails to provide direction, recognition, or purpose. Employees in such environments often feel disillusioned, unappreciated, and uninspired. There is no clear vision for the future, and employees often feel stuck in dead-end jobs without opportunities for growth or advancement. This can lead to burnout and resignation, where employees feel their hard work will never be acknowledged or rewarded.

6. Unchecked Greed and Materialism

The devil encourages greed, the desire for material gain at any cost, which often leads to exploitation, corruption, and spiritual emptiness. In 1 Timothy 6:10, Paul warns, "For the love of money is the root of all evil." Greed drives people to seek wealth and power at the expense of others. Greed in the workplace manifests in the form of unethical business practices, exploitative labor (such as low wages, lack of benefits, and unfair working conditions), and a disregard for employee well-being in favor of profits. Companies prioritizing shareholder value over their employees' health and dignity often create environments where employees are viewed as expendable assets, rather than as individuals with inherent worth. This leads to widespread dissatisfaction, resentment, and ongoing employee turnover.

The negative dynamics that we see in many workplaces today—deception, division, abuse of power, envy, greed, hopelessness, and exploitation—bear striking similarities to the evil works of the devil described in Christian scripture. These toxic forces harm individual employees and have long-lasting impacts on the company as a whole, leading to low morale, high turnover, and a damaged reputation.

Thanks to the power of social media platforms like Glassdoor, LinkedIn, and others, employees can now expose these toxic practices on a broad scale, revealing the unhealthy cultures that persist in some organizations. As more people become aware of these issues, there is a growing demand for organizations to adopt a more faith-centered, ethical approach to leadership—one that values honesty, empowerment, collaboration, and respect. In contrast to the works of the devil, a Christ-centered workplace culture emphasizes truth, unity, empowerment, compassion, and hope—values that lead to thriving organizations where employees and the business can flourish.

Chapter 11: Eternity

How would you define eternity? It is a profoundly thought-provoking question, and exploring the complexities of human nature, society, and organizational behavior is important. In truth, the vision of a perfect, Christ-centered workplace culture, where every principle taught by Jesus is entirely accepted and realized, is likely incomprehensible in its fullness for the current age. Despite being noble and transformative, here is why this vision will never fully manifest in our lifetime:

1. The Fallibility of Human Nature

At the heart of the issue lies human beings' fundamental nature. According to Christian doctrine, humanity has fallen from perfection due to sin, as narrated in the Genesis account of the Fall. This deeply embedded flaw manifests itself in selfishness, greed, pride, and fear that continue to shape human behaviors, even in professional environments. While individual human hearts can certainly experience growth, transformation, and moments of holiness, complete and consistent moral purity is elusive for everyone.

Workplaces, like all of society, are composed of imperfect people. Even well-meaning leaders will inevitably make mistakes, succumb to self-interest, or fail to embody the virtues of servant leadership that Jesus demonstrated. Leaders in high-powered positions may begin with ideals of servant leadership, only to find themselves ensnared by the systems they seek to transform (Keltner, 2017). The temptation to use power for personal gain, to compromise on integrity, or to control others rather than empower them is a recurring human challenge. Even if individual leaders and employees strive to live out Christ's teachings, businesses, corporations, and governments—are rarely structured around divine principles. The need for profit and competition primarily drives most businesses. The systemic issues built into corporate structures—such as hierarchies, power dynamics, capitalism, and economic inequalities—often counter the egalitarian and servant-driven ideals that Jesus espoused.

The workplace often operates in environments that emphasize self-promotion, individualism, and achievement, which can directly oppose the selflessness and humility that Jesus demonstrated. Even in organizations that genuinely attempt to center their practices on ethics, employees and leaders alike still face the daily temptation to promote their interests above those of others. This constant battle with ego ensures that the perfect Christlike work culture will always be aspirational but rarely realized. It is up to us to choose if we want to make a difference.

2. The Nature of the World and the Devil's Influence

According to Christian theology, the devil has a significant role in distorting human actions, leading people away from godly values, and spreading falsehood and division. In its current state, the world is not only governed by human sin but also influenced by spiritual forces of darkness that have long been at work. In Ephesians 6:12, Paul reminds us, "For our struggle is not against flesh and blood, but against the rulers, against the authorities, against the powers of this dark world and the spiritual forces of evil in the heavenly realms." The works of the devil—deception, manipulation, exploitation, division, and destruction—are woven into the fabric of every facet of human society, including our workplaces. Even with the best intentions, the world's spiritual battle works against the realization of Christ's perfect culture. The devil thrives on discord and conflict inherent in the systems of power and control that dominate the world today.

Many of the most powerful corporate entities in the world are built on practices that foster exploitation and manipulation. Whether through unfair labor practices, discrimination, or unethical competition, these systems often perpetuate the kind of toxic culture that directly opposes the unity and equality Christ desired for His followers. The devil's influence can be seen in how these companies prioritize profit over people and self-interest over collaboration. Even if individuals or companies seek to align with Christ's teachings, spiritual warfare complicates the journey. Christians are called to "take every thought captive" (2 Corinthians 10:5) and resist the enemy's temptations to act out of selfish ambition. However, the constant presence of hostile forces—whether through internal desires or external pressures—means that the full realization of Christ's ideal in workplaces is a battle that never fully ends on this side of eternity.

3. The Inevitability of Human Pride and Self-Interest

Human pride and self-interest are deeply ingrained traits that make the widespread realization of a Christ-centered work culture difficult, if not impossible, in our lifetime. One of the root causes of dysfunction in any organization is the natural tendency toward pride and self-exaltation. Jesus's teachings emphasize humility—that greatness comes through serving others (Mark 10:43-44). However, pride runs deep in the human heart. It is not just individuals in positions of power who are susceptible; employees at all levels struggle with selfish ambition and the desire for recognition, status, and control. This leads to manipulation, competition, and a lack of true collaboration.

The lust for power, control, and influence is another force in human society that corrupts even the most well-meaning individuals. Power can change people in ways that lead them to abuse or exploit others (Keltner, 2017). Corporate greed, the desire for status, and the pursuit of profit often trump the values of servant leadership and self-sacrifice that Jesus modeled. Once power structures become entrenched in society, they perpetuate themselves. Corporations, governments, and faith-based organizations can become institutionally corrupt over time, reinforcing values of individualism, competitiveness, and economic survival rather than community, equality, and humility. While individuals can change, entire systems take generations to transform, if at all.

4. The Influence of Economic Systems

Principles in modern economies stand in stark contrast to the values of Jesus. Capitalism, in particular, is founded on competition, scarcity, and profit maximization, which often require exploiting resources, including human labor. The capitalist model rewards those who innovate, compete, and dominate markets. It encourages behaviors driven by self-interest, greed, and competition, which counter Jesus's values of selflessness and generosity. Even if individuals within these systems want to live according to Christ's teachings, the economic pressure to "succeed" often leads them to compromise on their values.

Global capitalism is built on the premise of cheap labor and unregulated markets. Companies often cut costs by outsourcing jobs to countries where labor laws are lax, exploiting vulnerable populations. This exploitation is at odds with Jesus's call to love our neighbors and care for the marginalized. The scale of this systemic injustice is enormous and entrenched, making it incredibly difficult to build a Christ-centered global economic system within a single generation (Sennett, 2007).

5. The Shortness of Human Life and the Slow Pace of Change

Finally, there is the reality of human life: we are finite beings, and time is limited. It is nearly impossible for societal systems to transform fully in a single lifetime.

Change happens slowly. Even within the church, where followers of Christ are called to live out His teachings, the transformation journey is gradual. Christians desire to live out their faith with patience (Romans 12:12) and perseverance (James 1:12). The transformation of individuals and organizations to a truly Christlike culture is an ongoing process that will only see its fulfillment in the Kingdom of God.

Societal and workplace culture evolves over decades, if not centuries (Sennett, 2007). It is possible that in future generations, we may see a greater alignment between workplace cultures and Christian values, but immediate, large-scale change is improbable. Only the return of Christ and the establishment of God's perfect kingdom will bring about the complete transformation of society where justice, peace, equality, and love reign completely.

The full realization of a Christ-centered workplace culture—one where every individual embraces Jesus's teachings on humility, truth, service, peace, and unity—is not likely to happen in our lifetime. However, let's continue to pray otherwise.

Chapter 12: A Call to Reflect and Act

The Detroit Lions finished the 2024–2025 NFL Season with a record of 15-3, losing to the Washington Commanders in the Divisional Round of the playoffs. As we have examined the Detroit Lions' path to success, it becomes clear that their triumph is much more than strategy, talent, or even the thrill of winning games. Their story is one of cultivating an environment—an ecosystem of success—where individuals are not just seen as players on a team but as valued human beings with potential, ideas, and dignity. Their success does not solely lie in the Xs and Os of football but in how they build relationships, foster trust, and promote an atmosphere where everyone is empowered to grow, contribute, and ultimately flourish. This model is not just relevant to sports; it mirrors a philosophy of leadership, workplace culture, and personal integrity that aligns deeply with the teachings of Jesus Christ.

Throughout the life and example of Jesus, we see a leader who did not lead through domination or force but through service, humility, and love. His leadership was rooted in listening to others, valuing each person's worth, and encouraging them to be their best selves—whether in a public setting or in quiet personal moments. His message transcends time, providing a roadmap for creating communities, families, and workplaces centered on positive transformation and mutual respect. The principles we have uncovered from the Detroit Lions—unity, trust, selflessness, accountability, and mutual support—are not just tactics for success; they reflect the more profound truths we see in Jesus's teachings (Fry, 2003).

However, I want to challenge you, the reader, to go beyond the Lions' stories and the scripture's lessons. This is where the real work begins. Reflect deeply on your own life. How do you live each day? What do you truly value most—not just in words, but actions? How do these values shape how you show up in the world, both in the workplace and beyond? Are your daily behaviors aligned with the character you wish to develop? Moreover, are your actions contributing to an environment fostered by growth, collaboration, and positivity?

We often think of our behavior in broad strokes—maybe we pride ourselves on our honesty or hard work—but I invite you to consider the small, seemingly insignificant moments that form the fabric of your character. How do you treat others when no one is watching? How do you respond to challenging or stressful situations? Are you quick to listen, slow to anger, and quick to forgive? Do your actions align with the positive culture you wish to see around you?

Take a moment to examine both your public and private behaviors. Publicly, how do you interact with coworkers, friends, or even strangers? Do your words uplift and encourage, or do they tear down? Do you approach conflicts with a mindset of resolution and mutual understanding, or are you driven by ego and the need to be right? In private, do your habits reflect the same integrity and care that you outwardly express? Or do you slip into patterns of self-centeredness or complacency when no one is looking? Our character is shaped by our choices, not just the ones visible to others, but also the quiet decisions we make in solitude (Storr).

Consider, too, the broader impact of your efforts. We live in a world that often prioritizes quick success, external validation, and personal gain. However, true success—the success that builds long-lasting, positive workplaces and communities—is about more than accolades or recognition. It is about creating a culture where people can thrive. In the workplace context, it is about creating a space where employees are valued and allowed to reach their fullest potential. It is about fostering trust, where people feel safe to share ideas, take risks, and grow from their mistakes. It is about leading in a way that serves others and inspires them to do the same (Achor, 2018).

The Detroit Lions have modeled this kind of leadership and teamwork, and they have shown us that this environment of success is not just a product of top-down directives, but of shared responsibility and collective effort. Every player, coach, and staff member contributes to the overall culture. In the same way, every individual can influence the culture of their workplace or community. Whether you are the CEO or an entry-level employee, the boss or a team member, the energy you bring and the choices you make create a ripple effect (Blanchard, 2010).

An exemplary example of this was from Sheila Hamp's letter to Detroit Lions season ticket holders following the 2024–2025 season:

"Dear Lions Loyal Member,

This is not the letter I was hoping to write to you this year. It's not the ending we wanted or were expecting. The fact of the matter is this: we had a great year, a record-setting season, but fell short of our ultimate goal.

What never falls short is your support. I can't tell you how much I appreciate the support we have received from all of you, the city of Detroit and the entire state of Michigan. Ford Field is a legitimate home-field advantage, and that is because of you. It also felt like you gave us a home-field advantage in most of the away stadiums we played in this year. We appreciate you more than you will ever know. Your support continues to fuel us toward bigger things.

I am proud of the year we had. I am proud of our players, our coaches, our personnel department, and our entire staff, because at the Lions, we live the One Pride concept and truly win and lose together.

I know this weekend was difficult, and the next few weeks will be hard to watch as other teams walk the path we envisioned, but please know that we have never been more motivated. I know the future will look different, and the team that brought us so much success this year will never be together again. Pieces will change, but we are confident in where we are going and more aligned than ever as to how we get there.

One of the goals I set for our franchise was to create sustained success. The last two years have started that process. Back-to-back NFC North Division Championships and home playoff appearances are the type of successes that we envisioned, and we are on the path to continuing that.

Thank you for your continued support, thank you for donning your Honolulu Blue and thank you for continuing to be the driving force behind One Pride.

Go Lions!

Sheila Hamp"

So, I urge you to take this message to heart: the impact of your actions, big or small, can shape the environment around you. You can be a force for positive change, but it begins with you. It begins with looking inward and asking hard questions. Are you living in alignment with the values you claim to hold dear? Are you contributing to an atmosphere that supports others and invites them to succeed, or are you creating friction and division? As a leader, coach, or colleague, are you living out the principles of humility, respect, and care that you would like to see in the world?

This is where the challenge lies. It is not enough to agree with the principles we have discussed or to admire the culture of a successful team like the Lions. It is about taking action. It is about choosing every day to reflect the values that build trust, loyalty, and success in a significant way. It is about choosing to live with intentionality, build relationships rooted in compassion and integrity, and create spaces—whether in the workplace, your home, or your community—where people feel safe, valued, and empowered to grow.

As we have seen from the Detroit Lions' journey and the life of Jesus Christ, this work is not easy. It requires sacrifice, humility, and a commitment to something greater than ourselves. Nevertheless, it is also gratifying. The environment you help create, your impact on the people around you, and the legacy you leave behind will outlast any temporary success or individual achievement. It is about creating something lasting that transforms not just the workplace but lives.

So, I challenge you today to reflect. Take a hard look at your life, your character, your values, and your behaviors. Ask yourself: Are you living in a way that supports the kind of positive, thriving workplace and community you want to see? Are you willing to hold yourself accountable for the culture you help shape in public and private moments? Are you prepared to commit to this journey, not just for a day or a season, but for the long haul?

The power to create a better world, a more supportive and thriving environment, begins with you. You have everything within you to lead by example, make choices that reflect integrity, compassion, and purpose, and help build a space where everyone can thrive.

The journey toward a positive, thriving workplace starts with self-reflection but does not end there. It is a lifelong commitment to living out the values of service, humility, and love that we have discussed. Just like the Detroit Lions, you can be a leader who fosters a culture of success. You have the opportunity to make a difference. The choice is yours. Will you accept the challenge?

About the Author:

Adam Parsch is an author, Catholic Christian, husband, father, golfer, and customer success professional with over twenty years of experience in various client-facing roles. Born in Imlay City, Michigan, Adam has worked for organizations ranging from small startups to large enterprises, leading to him experiencing various environments across the United States. A skilled corporate strategist with a strong and respected history in customer success, Adam has built valuable enterprise-level relationships. He is known for his leadership, mentorship, and ability to inspire exceptional performance. His expertise extends across the Software as a Service space, where he fosters cross-functional alliances and drives growth through a mindset of continuous improvement.

Adam has had the unique opportunity to observe both human and corporate behavior within the dynamics of corporate America and in various places across the United States, Europe, Mexico, Canada, and the South Pacific. His reflections on these experiences, particularly how they align with the teachings of Jesus Christ, have profoundly influenced his personal and professional life.

His book, *Unmatched Grit*, was inspired by these reflections and the daily pursuit of living a Christlike life. Adam's hope is to share the lessons he's learned along the way and help others who may be facing similar challenges or seeking to live with greater purpose and resilience.

When he's not working, praying, or writing, Adam enjoys spending time with his small but mighty family—his wonderful wife and two children. If he finds any extra time on his hands, you'll likely find him on the golf course, playing basketball, spending time with friends, or enjoying the outdoors. Please feel free to follow and connect with Adam: https://www.linkedin.com/in/adamparsch

Index and References:

Preface:

Maleka, S. (2023). The Influence of Organisational Culture on the Implementation of Strategic Plans in a Public Service Organisations. ResearchGate. https://www.researchgate.net/publication/374752643

Saha, R., Cerchione, R., Singh, R., & Dahiya, R. (2020). Effect of ethical leadership and corporate social responsibility on firm performance: A systematic review. *Corporate Social Responsibility and Environmental Management, 27*(2), 409–429. https://onlinelibrary.wiley.com/doi/abs/10.1002/csr.1824

Chapter 1:

NFL Football Operations. (n.d.). *Detroit Lions*. NFL Football Operations. Retrieved February 21, 2025, from https://operations.nfl.com/learn-the-game/nfl-basics/team-histories/national-football-conference/north/detroit-lions/

Raj, K. M. (2023). Workplace Happiness: The Key to Employees Retention. *The Online Journal of Distance Education and E-Learning, 11*(2). https://tojdel.net/journals/tojdel/articles/v11i02b/v11i02b-108.pdf.

Shaheen, M. (2020, November 30). *Matt Patricia's Lions tenure riddled with disappointment from the start*. Pride of Detroit. https://www.prideofdetroit.com/2020/11/30/21724314/matt-patricia-tenure-riddled-disappointment

The Alternative Board. (2020, February 26). *"Culture Eats Strategy For Breakfast" - What Does it Mean?* Www.thealternativeboard.com. https://www.thealternativeboard.com/blog/culture-eats-strategy

Thomas, C. (2020, November 28). *Yes, Matt Patricia's Detroit Lions tenure was as bad as you think*. Detroit Free Press. https://eu.freep.com/story/sports/nfl/lions/2020/11/28/matt-patricia-fired-detroit-lions-marty-mornhinweg-rod-marinelli/6449725002/

Woodyard, E. (2024, January 26). *Dan Campbell links winless 2008 Lions to 2023 playoff run*. ESPN. https://www.espn.com/nfl/story/_/id/39379867/winless-2008-detroit-lions-enjoying-2023-lions-success-playoffs

Chapter 2:

Fitzgerald, A. (2020). Professional identity: A concept analysis. *Nursing Forum*, 55(3), 447–472. https://onlinelibrary.wiley.com/doi/abs/10.1111/nuf.12450

George, G., Haas, M. R., McGahan, A. M., Schillebeeckx, S. J. D., & Tracey, P. (2021). Purpose in the For-Profit Firm: A Review and Framework for Management Research. *Journal of Management*, 49(6), 014920632110064. https://doi.org/10.1177/01492063211006450

Chapter 3:

Brighton, S. (2024, December 19). *Lions Roar Back: Returning Players Poised for a Tech-Driven Future*. EWE's Tech Kitchen. https://angmv-mr.org/news-en/lions-roar-back-returning-players-poised-for-a-tech-driven-future/4172/

Fox, K. E., Johnson, S. T., Berkman, L. F., Sianoja, M., Soh, Y., Kubzansky, L. D., & Kelly, E. L. (2021). Organisational- and group-level workplace interventions and their effect on multiple domains of worker well-being: A systematic review. *Work & Stress*, 36(1), 1–30.

Gregory, S. (2024, December 9). *The Detroit Lions and the Detroit Workforce: A Tale of Transformation and Triumph*. Detroit Regional Partnership. https://www.detroitregionalpartnership.com/the-detroit-lions-and-the-detroit-workforce/

Join The Collective. (2024, February 8). *Embracing Unity: How Celebrating Cultural Diversity Enhances Workplace Inclusion*. Join the Collective. https://www.jointhecollective.com/article/celebrating-workplace-diversity-a-key-to-inclusion/

Chapter 4:

Dunne, T. (2024, December 20). *"It's going to be legendary:" Scottie Montgomery on why these Detroit Lions are built different*. Go Long. https://www.golongtd.com/p/its-going-to-be-legendary-scottie

Keefer, Z. (2025, January 15). The genius of Dan Campbell: "He's the best leader I've ever been around." *The New York Times*. https://www.nytimes.com/athletic/6047743/2025/01/15/dan-campbell-detroit-lions-coach-leader-nfl-playoffs

Payton, M. (2022, June 14). *How does Lions owner Sheila Hamp compare to other, successful NFL owners?* Pride of Detroit. https://www.prideofdetroit.com/2022/6/14/23164038/detroit-lions-owner-sheila-hamp-compared-successful-nfl-owners

Raven, B. (2022, April 15). *Lions GM Brad Holmes credits team's dedication to diversity, talks NFL draft on ex-Falcons GM's podcast.* MLive. https://www.mlive.com/lions/2022/04/lions-gm-brad-holmes-credits-teams-dedication-to-diversity-talks-nfl-draft-on-ex-falcons-gms-podcast.html

Woodyard, E. (2025, January 20). *Coach Dan Campbell says Lions will 'come back stronger'.* ESPN. https://www.espn.co.uk/nfl/story/_/id/43492843/coach-dan-campbell-says-lions-gonna-come-back-stronger

Chapter 5:

Baldoni, J. (2023, September 15). Sheila Ford Hamp: How To Lead When You Own The Team. *Forbes.* https://www.forbes.com/sites/johnbaldoni/2023/09/14/sheila-ford-hamp-how-to-lead-when-you-own-the-team/

Birkett, D. (2021, January 24). *Dan Campbell may be "the only guy that can resurrect" the Detroit Lions. Here's why.* Detroit Free Press. https://eu.freep.com/story/sports/nfl/lions/2021/01/24/detroit-lions-coach-dan-campbell-leader/6685308002/

Broder, M. (2023, March 26). *Taylor Decker: Pride of the Lions.* Woodward Sports Network. https://wp.woodwardsports.com/stories/taylor-decker-pride-of-the-lions/

Maakaron, J. (2023, August 17). *Presence of Frank Ragnow Important for Lions' Offensive Line.* Detroit Lions on SI; Sports Illustrated. https://www.si.com/nfl/lions/news/presence-of-frank-ragnow-important-lions-offensive-line

Chapter 6:

Beresford, C. (2021, January 19). *It's Official: Fiat Chrysler and PSA Group Are Now Stellantis.* Car and Driver. https://www.caranddriver.com/news/a35254008/fiat-chrysler-peugeot-become-stellantis/

Cavaiani, A. C. (2015). *Detroit's Sport Spaces And The Rhetoric Of Consumption.* DigitalCommons@WayneState. https://digitalcommons.wayne.edu/oa_dissertations/1307/

General Motors. (n.d.). *Learn More About GM's Vision.* General Motors. https://www.gm.com/company/about-us

Lewis, D. L. (1976). *The Public Image of Henry Ford: An American Folk Hero and His Company.* Wayne State University Press.

Womack, J. P., Jones, D. T., & Roos, D. (2007). *The Machine That Changed the World*. Simon & Schuster.

Chapter 7:

Chang, C.-H., Lin, H.-W., Tsai, W.-H., Wang, W.-L., & Huang, C.-T. (2021). Employee Satisfaction, Corporate Social Responsibility and Financial Performance. *Sustainability*, *13*(18), 9996. https://doi.org/10.3390/su13189996

Deal, T. E., & Kennedy, A. A. (2008). *The New Corporate Cultures: Revitalizing the Workplace After Downsizing, Mergers, and Reengineering*. Basic Books.

Kotter, J. P., & Heskett, J. L. (2011). *Corporate Culture and Performance*. Free Press.

Chapter 8:

Chala, N., Poplavska, O., Danylevych, N., Ievseitseva, O., & Sova, R. (2022). Intrinsic motivation of millennials and generation Z in the new post-pandemic reality. *Problems and Perspectives in Management*, *20*(2), 536–550. https://doi.org/10.21511/ppm.20(2).2022.44

Darby, M. (2023). *"I've chosen out of this world": Once again, Chris Pratt defends his religious beliefs*. Deseret News. https://www.deseret.com/faith/2023/5/8/23715359/chris-pratt-defends-religious-beliefs-faith-christian/

Marshall, P. D. (2014). *Celebrity and Power*. University of Minnesota Press.

Mastro, G. (2024). *Three things to learn from Russell Brand's conversion to Catholicism*. The Saint Anselm Crier. https://criernewsroom.com/opinion/2024/09/12/three-things-to-learn-from-russell-brands-conversion-to-catholicism/

Wollard, K. K. (2011). Quiet Desperation: Another Perspective on Employee Engagement. *Advances in Developing Human Resources*, *13*(4), 526–537. https://doi.org/10.1177/1523422311430942

Chapter 9:

Henry, C. D., & Shannon, L. (2023). *Virtual Natives: How a New Generation is Revolutionizing the Future of Work, Play, and Culture*. John Wiley & Sons.

Zemke, R., Raines, C., & Filipczak, B. (2013). *Generations at Work: Managing the Clash of Boomers, Gen Xers, and Gen Yers in the Workplace*. American Management Association.

Chapter 10:

Jones M. (2003). Overcoming the myth of free will in criminal law: the true impact of the genetic revolution. *Duke Law Journal, 52*(5), 1031–1053.

Roskies, A. (2006). Neuroscientific challenges to free will and responsibility. *Trends in Cognitive Sciences, 10*(9), 419–423. https://doi.org/10.1016/j.tics.2006.07.011

Chapter 11:

Keltner, D. (2017). *The Power Paradox: How We Gain and Lose Influence.* Penguin Books.

Sennett, R. (2007). *The Culture of the New Capitalism.* Yale University Press.

Chapter 12:

Achor, S. (2018). *The Happiness Advantage: How a Positive Brain Fuels Success in Work and Life.* Crown.

Blanchard, K. (2010). *Leading at a Higher Level: Blanchard on Leadership and Creating High Performing Organizations.* FT Press.

Fry, L. W. (2003). Toward a theory of spiritual leadership. *The Leadership Quarterly, 14*(6), 693–727. https://doi.org/10.1016/j.leaqua.2003.09.001

www.ingramcontent.com/pod-product-compliance
Lightning Source LLC
Chambersburg PA
CBHW032327270325
24233CB00005B/73